"*Sabbath Keeping* is not just a gentle and info..............., it is an inspiration. Without question, this is the best book I've read in years on the art and discipline of keeping sabbath. We live in an age of hurry, an age of multitasking and stress; we could not need Lynne Baab's book more."

LAUREN F. WINNER, AUTHOR OF *GIRL MEETS GOD* AND *MUDHOUSE SABBATH*

"Finally we have a book on the sabbath that avoids the polemics of sabbath law and recovers the biblical and practical experience of sabbath rest. Lynne Baab reminds us that we do not just keep the sabbath as a religious ritual, but the sabbath keeps us as a gracious gift of renewal. Regardless of one's tradition, this is a book that will provide both a theological and practical guide for creating an intentional sabbath experience. This is a 'one size fits all' prescription for maintaining spiritual fitness in a secular culture running at a 24-7 rate. Read it, practice it, and find rest for your soul."

RAY S. ANDERSON, SENIOR PROFESSOR OF THEOLOGY AND MINISTRY, FULLER THEOLOGICAL SEMINARY

"Lynne Baab is passionate about the sabbath. Having personally experienced the spiritual enrichment of sabbath keeping, she writes to entice the reader to gratefully accept God's gracious invitation to sabbath rest and renewal. She explores Jewish and Christian sabbath traditions and writings, plus practices of her friends and her family, in this gentle yet challenging book that is practical and practicable. It comes from her heart and will speak to yours. It could change your lifestyle and enhance your relationship with God!"

REV. DON POSTEMA, AUTHOR OF *CATCH YOUR BREATH* AND *SPACE FOR GOD*

"Every voice prodding us to keep the sabbath in these hectic times is urgently needed. Lynne Baab's voice is clear; her suggestions apply to a great diversity of people; her own practice offers an excellent model. Keeping the sabbath changed my life; I pray that you too know the freedom of its rest."

MARVA DAWN, AUTHOR OF *KEEPING THE SABBATH WHOLLY* AND *UNFETTERED HOPE*

"Sabbath is not just a day off. It is a way of life, a gift of grace. To rest, to sabbath, to stop—these are ways of acknowledging and receiving that gift. Drawing from the wisdom of the best thinkers on this subject and her own deep experience of the power in 'stopping,' Lynne Baab guides us to a place of rest. She exhorts us to walk in the 'rhythms of rest,' and to realize that keeping sabbath is a way of affirming the deep love of God that cannot be earned through frenetic activity. I recommend this practical and life-giving book."

KERI WYATT KENT, AUTHOR OF *GOD'S WHISPER IN A MOTHER'S CHAOS, THE GARDEN OF THE SOUL* AND *BREATHE: CREATING SPACE FOR GOD IN A HECTIC LIFE*

"Dorothy Bass once wrote that the commandment to observe sabbath is the only one people brag about breaking—being busy is equated with being significant. Lynne Baab has rediscovered the gift of sabbath keeping and offers wise counsel on the importance of doing nothing."

JOHN ORTBERG, AUTHOR OF *IF YOU WANT TO WALK ON WATER, YOU'VE GOT TO GET OUT OF THE BOAT*

"I've tried many times to be a better sabbath keeper—but I'm just too busy. And so are my family and friends. We've made a virtue out of being overworked and then rationalizing that as faithfulness. Lynne Baab's book not only called me up short but also called me back to a biblically sound and graciously practical reconsideration of God's gift of sabbath. This is the best book on sabbath that I've seen, and my life is changing after having read it."

DR. STEPHEN A. HAYNER, COLUMBIA THEOLOGICAL SEMINARY

"I chose to read this manuscript out of sheer longing and delight because the idea and the reality of sabbath keeping is so compelling to me these days. It is a wonderful book that articulates all the questions that we wonder about and then explores the sabbath as a discipline that soon becomes one of God's greatest gifts to us as human beings. It is a gift that is, as Lynne so eloquently describes it, full of grace, freedom and abundance. Reading this book made me love God more because he thought to craft a gift that is so beautiful and extravagant but also so practical and necessary. The sabbath is a discipline that will save our lives."

RUTH HALEY BARTON, COFOUNDER OF THE TRANSFORMING CENTER, SPIRITUAL DIRECTOR, AUTHOR OF *INVITATION TO SOLITUDE AND SILENCE*

K E E P I N G

FINDING FREEDOM IN THE RHYTHMS OF REST

Lynne M. Baab

IVP Books

An imprint of InterVarsity Press
Downers Grove, Illinois

InterVarsity Press
P.O. Box 1400, Downers Grove, IL 60515-1426
World Wide Web: www.ivpress.com
E-mail: email@ivpress.com

InterVarsity Press® is the book-publishing division of InterVarsity Christian Fellowship/USA®, a movement of
students and faculty active on campus at hundreds of universities, colleges and schools of nursing in the United
States of America, and a member movement of the International Fellowship of Evangelical Students. For
information about local and regional activities, write Public Relations Dept., InterVarsity Christian Fellowship/
USA, 6400 Schroeder Rd., P.O. Box 7895, Madison, WI 53707-7895, or visit the IVCF website at
<www.intervarsity.org>.

Design: Cindy Kiple
Images: Darrell Gulin/Getty Images

ISBN 978-0-8308-3258-3

Printed in the United States of America ∞

InterVarsity Press is committed to protecting the environment and to the responsible use of
natural resources. As a member of the Green Press Initiative we use recycled paper whenever
possible. To learn more about the Green Press Initiative, visit <www.greenpressinitiative.org>.

Library of Congress Cataloging-in-Publication Data

Baab, Lynne M.
  Sabbath keeping: finding freedom in the rhythms of rest / Lynne M.
Baab.
    p. cm.
  Includes bibliograhical references (p.
  ISBN 0-8308-3258-0 (pbk.: alk. paper)
  1. Ten commandments—Sabbath. 2. Rest—Religious
aspects—Christianity. 3. Sabbath. I. Title.
  BV4670.B33 2005
  263'.3—dc22
                                                                                2004022166

P   23   22   21   20   19   18   17   16   15   14   13   12   11   10   9   8   7
Y   25   24   23   22   21   20   19   18   17   16   15   14   13   12

Contents

Acknowledgments

More than one hundred people talked to me—in person, by phone or by e-mail—about the sabbath. They come from all over the United States and some other countries as well, and they span a wide range of ages and Christian traditions. I am grateful for their thoughts. I am able to give so many practical suggestions in this book because of the people who took the time to respond to my questions. I thank them all.

I am also indebted to the people who have gone before me as writers about the sabbath. Their insights have shaped my understanding of my own long-held sabbath habit. I knew the sabbath blessed me, but I wasn't sure how to articulate my experiences until I began reading books on the sabbath.

One author to whom I am particularly grateful is Don Postema. He allowed me to interview him when he came to Seattle, and I am still thinking about the things we talked about.

I am also thankful for the people who read my manuscript and made helpful suggestions: Anne Baumgartner, Joleen Burgess, Rev. Doug Early and Rev. Claudia M. Rowe. Dave Zimmerman, my editor at InterVarsity Press, helped me improve the book in many ways. My husband, Dave Baab, has been my loving sabbath partner for more than twenty-five years, and he also helped me with the manuscript. I'm grateful to him for that and much more.

CHAPTER ONE

A Gift for Our Time

Remember the sabbath day, and keep it holy. Six days you shall labor and do all your

work. But the seventh day is a sabbath to the LORD your God; you shall not do any work.

. . . For in six days the LORD made heaven and earth, the sea, and all that is in them,

but rested the seventh day.

EXODUS 20:8-11

I didn't know I was allowed to rest."

I heard these words from a mother with young children just after I had spoken to a Mothers of Preschoolers group about the sabbath. During the discussion time, many of the moms talked about the seven-day-a-week pressure they feel to keep countless balls in the air. They drive their kids to activities, keep the home front organized and clean, fix meals, shop for food and kids' clothes and toys and school supplies, and try to give their children a significant amount of undivided attention. Many of them also work part time or full time for pay. They multitask continually, and they find it exhausting.

I could see wistful smiles on the women's faces when I de-

scribed my own sabbath observance during the years when I'd had
young children. I talked about how one day each week I chose not
to do housework or run er-
rands. On that day, my husband and I could play with our
kids or take them to a park
without worrying about the
other things we needed to do.

Our culture invariably supposes that

action and accomplishment are

better than rest, that doing

something—anything—is better than

doing nothing.

WAYNE MULLER, *SABBATH*

"I didn't know I was al-
lowed to rest."

What's going on in our culture, in our world, that a
mother with young children
believes she's supposed to be
active and productive every minute? Why is it scary to think about
stopping or slowing down all this relentless activity? Why do we
need to justify our existence by constant motion? Why would we
think we aren't allowed to rest?

The sabbath has been a great gift to me by slowing me down
and inviting me to experience God's rest—not just analyze it. Jesus
said to his disciples, "Come to me, all you that are weary and are
carrying heavy burdens, and I will give you rest. Take my yoke
upon you, and learn from me; for I am gentle and humble in heart,
and you will find rest for your souls" (Mt 11:28-29). I have received that gift of rest in Christ because of the sabbath.

The sabbath has also enabled me to learn from Jesus, to take his
gentle yoke on my shoulders rather than live in response to the
world's demands and my own unhealthy desires. Keeping a sabbath has taught me the deep truths of God's love as much as any
faith discipline I have observed as an adult. It has shaped my heart,

opening me to receive God's gifts more fully. The sabbath has inscribed God's grace on my soul in a way I can barely describe.

I stumbled into sabbath keeping because I experienced it while living in Israel many years ago. My commitment to the sabbath didn't come from theological conviction, guilt or any outside force. I experienced it, felt it was a gift and believed God wanted me to experience that gift every week. I'm glad it happened that way.

CONFUSION ABOUT THE SABBATH

What is the sabbath? A weekly day of rest and worship. A day to cease working and relax in God's care for us. A day to stop the things that occupy our workdays and participate in activities that nurture peace, worship, relationships, celebration and thankfulness. The purpose of the sabbath is to clear away the distractions of our lives so we can rest in God and experience God's grace in a new way.

Some people find the sabbath confusing. The idea raises so many questions that they have decided not to observe a sabbath or to ignore the issue as much as possible. Some of the questions are theological. When we observe a sabbath, aren't we falling into Old Testament legalism? Didn't Jesus come to fulfill the law? Doesn't that mean we no longer have to observe a sabbath?

The practical questions can be equally confusing. Even if we want to keep a sabbath, when should we do it? Some Christians say that Sunday parallels the Saturday sabbath for Jews and that we must keep Sunday special because Jesus rose from the dead on "the first day of the week." Other Christians say the Saturday sabbath is still mandated by God. Some people work on Saturday and Sunday. Are they violating God's law? Can they observe a sabbath on a weekday?

Adding to the confusion is the question of what to do and what not to do on the sabbath. The 1982 movie *Chariots of Fire* was based on the true story of Eric Liddell, a devout Christian who eventually became a missionary to China. In his early twenties, he was selected to run for Great Britain in the 1912 Olympics. His initial heat was scheduled for a Sunday, and he refused to compete. His story made front-page news. Britain was up in arms about his decision.

If we set out to keep a sabbath, should we refuse to engage in sporting activities as Eric Liddell did? Is a bike ride different from competing in organized sports? What about playing tennis or swimming with your kids? Going for a long walk?

The Old Testament rules about the sabbath centered around a day of rest from work. In our world, what constitutes work? Reading and answering e-mail? Balancing the checkbook? Cooking? Shopping for groceries? Doing a little home remodeling project? Mowing the lawn and pulling up weeds? Getting organized for the week ahead? The Bible acknowledges that some kinds of work are necessary even on the sabbath. Children need to be cared for, cows need to be milked and animals need to be pulled out of pits. How do we know if we are tending to genuine needs rather than slipping into patterns that inflate our sense of self-importance?

SABBATH PRACTICES

A growing number of people have found answers to these questions, answers that work for them. They have established sabbath patterns that nurture intimacy with God. They have experimented with a variety of habits for the one day, in order to see which observances enable them to live in grace the other six days.

The variety of sabbath possibilities is amazing. A university student loves to wear a dress to church. Then she stays in her dress through the evening to remind herself that this is a special day. Even something as mundane as breakfast cereal can mark a day of rest. A couple prepares steel-cut oats on Sunday mornings because the meal takes so long to cook. The gift of the sabbath is the gift of abundant time, and a slow-cooking breakfast helps this couple step outside their daily routine of schedules and hurrying.

Some people nurture particular Bible study and prayer habits for their sabbath. One business owner saves up the homework for his Bible study class and does it all after church on Sunday, his sabbath. He admits that he enjoys letting the assignments pile up, because then he's motivated to spend time in the Scriptures on Sunday afternoons. Another man, a Bible school teacher and administrator, says he devotes Sunday afternoons to intercessory prayer. Whenever he gets an e-mail with a prayer request, he prints it out and sets it aside for Sundays. He enjoys reading back over those prayer requests and praying in a leisurely fashion on his sabbath.

> A sabbath to me is a day of rest from the modern-day craziness of life.
>
> CRAIG, A MAN IN HIS TWENTIES

One family observes a sabbath that begins on Saturday in the late afternoon and goes until just before dinner on Sunday. They begin their sabbath with a family gathering that includes a breath prayer. "Breathe out your frustrations and worries into the presence of God," the father or mother says. "Breathe in God's presence. God is as near as the air you breathe." This prayer has become so special to the kids that if the parents forget the breath prayer, the kids remind them.

SOLD OUT ON THE SABBATH

Wayne, an ad agency writer in his midthirties, began observing a sabbath a few years ago, motivated both by obedience to God and by a sense that a day of rest is a commonsense thing to do. He has concentrated on making his sabbath different from the other days of the week. On Sundays he tries not to do anything related to his job. He goes to church, does fun things with his family and sometimes does nothing.

If you work seven 50-hour weeks in a row, you'll get no more done than if you worked seven 40-hour weeks in a row.

STUDY CITED IN *THE SEATTLE TIMES*, AUGUST 24, 2003

He occasionally works in the yard or runs errands. He says he is willing to do this kind of work on his sabbath because errands and chores don't demand from him the same energy and focus of his job. In fact, some of these activities are relaxing and meditative.

Wayne has found that when he does a little work for his job on Sunday in order to be better off when the workweek starts, it doesn't do the trick. Instead, his week is harried and difficult, and he feels chronically behind. In contrast, when he doesn't work on Sundays, even when he feels he needs to, he has a better week following.

"It's weird," he notes. "But I think I can guess why this happens. First, God knows me better than I know myself. He made the sabbath for me. When I live the way he tells me to, I'm simply operating in the most optimal, efficient way. The day of rest gives me more energy, focus and ability. If you change your oil according to the manufacturer's specs, your car works better."

Wayne also believes our obedience triggers a touch of the

miraculous. "God honors our obedience," he says. "When in faith I decide not to work, even though all my data tells me that a few hours spent on Sunday will save time later on, God makes things happen—probably thousands of small, hardly noticeable things—so that I come out ahead."

Wayne compares sabbath keeping to tithing, observing that when people give away ten percent of their income in obedience to God, their finances just work out better. He also cites the Israelites in the wilderness. When they followed the manna-gathering schedule as instructed, they always had enough—even though that meant manna behaved inconsistently, staying good for an extra day to cover the sabbath, rotting in the same amount of time on other days. Sabbath keeping works the same way, giving a gift of time that we often can't figure out logically.

Wayne is one of many people who talked to me about how they get more done during the weeks when they observe a sabbath. The rhythm of work and rest seems to help us function more purposefully and energetically, living in responsive obedience to the pattern God designed for us.

> Just as tithing reminds me that all I have is from God, so sabbath keeping reminds me that God is in control.
>
> SUSAN, A MOM IN HER LATE THIRTIES

SIMPLY BELOVED, A CHILD OF GOD

Ann, single and in her early fifties, is another enthusiastic sabbath keeper. She has observed a sabbath for thirty-three years, ever since she was in college. Over the years, her sabbath has occurred on various days, depending on her work schedule. Currently her sabbath is on Friday because she works in a church.

Ann begins her sabbath on Thursday evening and usually continues resting through Friday evening, so her weekly sabbath is actually a little longer than twenty-four hours. As she has gotten older, she has found she needs that much rest in order to cope with the stresses of the other days of the week and to work productively.

On her sabbath, Ann ceases working on anything that might have appeared on a "to do" list earlier in the week: all work, all thoughts of work, all chores and household details. She acknowledges that this routine took many months of practice in her first year of observance, but it is now almost automatic. If she finds "life" intruding into her sabbath, that's a sign of serious stress and triggers remedial action.

She takes the day as a gift, a day to do anything in the presence of God. Her sabbath often involves fiction, ferry rides and saltwater beaches. Because she can't observe the sabbath on Sunday, public worship is seldom involved, so in that sense the day is incomplete, she says.

Ann reflects on her day of rest:

> I began observing a sabbath because someone convinced me it was a biblical command and linked it to wonderful promises. I have continued to observe a sabbath because I have experienced it as my greatest joy. On that day I am not "Ann the _____" (insert various roles and titles). On that day I am a disciple, not a leader. On that day I am beloved, simply beloved.
>
> In the early years, I felt I had truly kept the sabbath if I reached that moment when my active life identity fell away and I was just a child of God. In these later years, it's not a struggle to enter into that state. Being a child of God, and

only a child of God, feels like old clothes that I slip into with relief for those hours each week.

The sabbath is one of those gospel duties that absolutely convinces us of the goodness of God. The more we practice it, the greater a privilege it becomes, the more essential it feels, the deeper it connects us to the river of life that provides fruit in all seasons.

What a wonderful God we worship, whose creative work models a day of rest that is sweet to the ones created. "It is very good." What a gift is human life on earth, set in relationships. We've been given good work worth doing, done with gusto for six days, celebrated with a sigh and song on the seventh day. The sabbath-keeping command is like the promise, "O taste and see that the Lord is good."

THE SABBATH AND GRACE

Recently I was talking with a friend about a biblical passage on grace: Ephesians 2:1-10. In that passage, the apostle Paul insists that apart from Christ we are dead, and in Christ we receive love, mercy and new life. All this comes to us as a gift, the gift of grace. We cannot do anything to earn it. My friend asked me if I ever truly experienced God's grace. As I thought about her question, I realized that the sabbath, more than anything else, has enabled me to experience this grace that comes to us in Christ.

The sabbath teaches us grace because it connects us experientially to the basic truth that nothing we do will earn God's love. As long as we are working hard, using our gifts to serve others, experiencing joy in our work along with the toil, we are always in danger of believing that our actions trigger God's love for us. Only in stopping, really stopping, do we teach our hearts and souls that we are loved apart from what we do.

During a day of rest, we have the chance to take a deep breath and look at our lives. God is at work every minute of our days, yet we seldom notice. Noticing requires intentional stopping, and the sabbath provides that opportunity. On the sabbath we can take a moment to see the beauty of a maple leaf, created with great care by our loving Creator. We can slow down long enough to observe the loveliness of our child's face or our friend's smile. On the sabbath, perhaps while taking a walk or waking from a nap, we can reflect on the previous week and notice a particular way God acted in our lives or answered a prayer. All these gifts come to us from the hand of God, and taking time to notice them helps us remember the generosity of the giver.

> Why do I observe a sabbath?
>
> Because the Scriptures encourage us to do so. Because I need time to recharge the human batteries. Because I need and want to worship with others on a regular basis.
>
> SAM, A RETIRED MINISTER IN HIS SEVENTIES

The sabbath teaches grace because it invites us to rest and rejoice in what we have, rather than focus on what we do not have. The sabbath invites us to practice thankfulness. On workdays we have to think about what we don't have and what we need to do. On the sabbath we can forget all that and simply enjoy what is.

Our culture is obsessed with production, possession and accomplishment. The sabbath invites us to spend a day apart from the media's incessant cry of "More!" The sabbath invites us into a rhythm, a structure, that frees us from outside pressures. And that freedom communicates God's grace to us.

The sabbath gives us time to reflect. What do I really care about? What are my deepest feelings and longings? In what areas of life do I need God the most? What do I need to confess to God? What do I need to explore that has great potential for growth? Who am I, anyway? Why am I here? What purpose does God have for my life? What purpose do I desire for my life? Bringing our innermost feelings into the open can teach us deep grace as we grow in understanding that God accepts us completely, forgiving us for the sin we find and helping us grow in our sense of purpose and direction.

Without time to stop, we cannot notice God's hand in our lives, practice thankfulness, step outside our culture's values or explore our deepest longings. Without time to rest, we will seriously undermine our ability to experience God's unconditional love and acceptance. The sabbath is a gift whose blessings cannot be found anywhere else.

When I take a break once a week, I remember that God is the one in charge of keeping the world turning and not me. Taking a day off each week also encourages me to be responsible with how I spend my time on the other six days.

CHRIS, A WOMAN IN HER TWENTIES

FRIENDSHIP WITH GOD

The sabbath nurtures relationships. The fast pace of our world encourages us to forget that relationships take time. Friendship is a slow art, whether it's with God, family members or other people.

The sabbath can give us precious and much-needed time to grow in friendship, to have leisurely conversations that help us go deeper with the people we love and with God. Loving and being loved bring grace into our lives.

As people near the end of life, they usually engage in a kind of review, examining their regrets about how they lived. "I worked too hard," many people say. "I was a stranger to my kids when they were little, and I wish I had spent more time with my spouse."

In the same way, our own hard work and busy pace can make us strangers to God. Catholic theologian Leonard Doohan believes that without the reflection and meditation that come from regularly stopping our activity, "we lose a sense of God or drag an outmoded image along behind us." Our relationship with God gets stuck, and we deny ourselves the opportunity to let our childish views of God grow into a real relationship, full of depth and wonder and mystery.

Doohan continues, "To fail to see the value of simply being with God and 'doing nothing' is to miss the heart of Christianity. . . . If in life we are not still, cannot be inspired by the beauty around us, cannot concentrate or be silent, how then can we suddenly achieve this in prayer?" Prayer and contemplation grow out of patterns of quiet and leisure. We want to bring our concerns to God, confess our sins and draw near to him in prayer, but we are expecting something impossible if we do not also allow ourselves to "do nothing" and rest in quietness from time to time.

The sabbath provides a structure to build "doing nothing" into our schedules. This kind of rest provides a foundation for deeper prayer and continued growth in friendship with God because it nurtures within us the stillness and silence that are essential to prayer.

Sabbath Issues and Stories

We will continue to consider how the sabbath connects with prayer, Christian growth and grace as we proceed through this book. We will look at the biblical commands regarding the sabbath, evaluating the way Christians today are called to respond. We will explore patterns of sabbath observance for different ages and stages of life: for single people, families with young children, students and empty nesters. Two of the biggest sabbath questions are, "What shall I cease from doing on the sabbath?" and "What shall I do on the sabbath?" We will look at many options for both.

We will hear from a variety of voices. As I tell people's sabbath stories, I will change the names and some of the identifying details. As a beginning foundation, in the next chapter I will tell you my own story.

Questions for Reflection, Discussion and Journaling

1. What do you remember from your childhood about the sabbath? What positive models do you remember? What negative models?

2. When you consider slowing down for one day each week, what obstacles and fears do you find in your heart? What do you imagine might be a positive result of keeping a sabbath?

3. What questions do you have about sabbath keeping?

Praying About the Sabbath

Spend some time praying about your fears and your questions about the sabbath. Ask God to meet you and answer you. Ask him to attune your spiritual ears so you can hear his invitation to rest, and to open your heart so you can respond.

What Happens When Everything Stops

For by grace you have been saved through faith, and this is not your own doing; it is the gift of God—not the result of works, so that no one may boast.

EPHESIANS 2:8-9

I bumped into the sabbath quite by accident. It happened because my husband, Dave, and I spent two years in the Middle East more than twenty years ago.

Our weekly rhythm got scrambled because the day off in that part of the world is either Friday or Saturday, depending on whether you are in a Jewish or Muslim area. Our options were significantly reduced that day, and having nothing to do one day each week began to have its own appeal. We learned to rest, and we learned that rest is one of God's great gifts to humans. We have never been the same.

THE FIRST STEP

From the time Dave and I began talking about marriage, we also discussed living overseas. Dave had trained as a specialist in a narrow area of dentistry and was teaching in a dental school in Seattle. People told us we could probably go anywhere in the world, even countries closed to missionaries, because of his particular skill.

Two years into our marriage we moved to Iran, intending to live there several years. Dave had an appealing contract at a dental school in the southern city of Shiraz, and before we left home we studied the language in preparation for a long stay. I got a job teaching English in a nursing school. It was the late 1970s, and we had no idea that the Iranian revolution was on the horizon. We ended up staying in Iran only six months.

Although our time there was short, Iran was where we began seeing the week in a different light. With Friday being the Muslim holy day, the workweek began on Saturday. Sunday was just another workday, as were Monday, Tuesday and Wednesday. On Thursday everyone worked a half day, and Friday was completely free.

We worshiped with the only Christian congregation in Shiraz, an Anglican church with two services, one in English and one in Farsi, the Persian language. Both services were held on Sunday evenings in a charming building that blended traditional church architecture with Iranian decorative tile. As we walked into that lovely church each Sunday evening, I began to understand the significance of Sunday as the day to celebrate the resurrection of Jesus. Even if Sunday was a busy workday, most Christians around the world were gathering for worship on the day of resurrection, also called the Lord's Day.

As we experienced this new weekly rhythm in Iran, and as the weeks and months rolled by, increasing violence around Iran indicated that all was not well. In early 1979, foreigners were advised to leave the country. We went to Israel on vacation, expecting these troubles to be short-lived. Through an amazing series of relational connections, Dave was offered a job at a dental school in Tel Aviv. He accepted the job when it became clear that things in Iran were not going to settle down anytime soon. We found ourselves living in Israel for a year and a half, something we had never expected.

I was delighted at the prospect of visiting biblical sites. I expected that seeing these places firsthand would somehow transform my relationship with God. I had no idea that, of all the things we experienced in Israel, the sabbath would have the greatest impact.

ANOTHER WEEKLY RHYTHM

The weekly pattern in Israel was only slightly different from what we had experienced in Iran. Now the workweek began on Sunday morning. On Sundays in Israel, my husband headed off to the university to begin his week of teaching. I decided to put off looking for a job because I wanted to study Hebrew intensively. My daily classes began on Sunday morning.

We worked and studied all day Sunday through Thursday. Friday was a half day of work. Sometime between noon and two o'clock on Friday afternoon, people left work, shopped in preparation for the sabbath, and settled into a different mental and emotional space.

The Jewish sabbath begins at sundown Friday and lasts until sundown Saturday. During that time, stores, restaurants and movie theaters were closed in Jewish neighborhoods like ours, and throughout Israel the buses didn't run.

Again we became involved in a small Christian congregation that met on Sunday evening. Saturday was not possible as a time of worship because so many of us came on buses. Just as in Iran, our corporate worship experience was connected to the Lord's Day, the day of Jesus' resurrection, when most of us had been working all day.

STOPPING

We lived on the top floor of a typical four-story Israeli apartment building. (Of course, the bomb shelter on the ground floor didn't seem typical to us!) Dave's salary didn't stretch far, and electricity was expensive, so we seldom ran our air conditioning. The sliding doors leading to our balcony were open almost every day of the year, as were all our windows. When we found our apartment, we hadn't realized the challenge of its location, just two buildings away from the main road leading north out of Tel Aviv. We endured incredible traffic noise coming through our open windows as the buses, trucks and myriad cars thundered north all day and night.

The first effect of the Jewish sabbath we noticed was the unbelievable silence on Friday evening and all day Saturday. No buses. Trucks stopped transporting goods. Few people drove their cars. The silence was like fresh water flowing into our lives.

We quickly made friends with people our age from other English-speaking countries. We didn't have a car, but most of our friends did, so in our first months in Israel we usually went on outings with friends on Saturdays. After a few months, however, I became pregnant. I didn't feel well for much of the pregnancy, which dramatically curtailed the weekly outings. That's when our real experience of the sabbath began.

What can you do when no stores or restaurants or movie theaters are open? How can you find entertainment when you don't have a car, the buses aren't running, and friends with cars aren't coming to pick you up? We didn't own a TV or computer. We lived three or four miles from the beach—too far to walk for a swim. Jaffa, the Arab part of Tel Aviv where stores and restaurants were open on Saturday, was even farther away. There was simply nothing to do.

I learned that the Hebrew word for sabbath means "stop." Often in the Bible it is translated as "rest," an equally valid translation, but to me the word *rest* has overtones of something different than "stop." Life really did stop for us on Friday evening and Saturday in Tel Aviv.

> The meaning of the Sabbath is to celebrate time rather than space.
>
> Six days a week we live under the tyranny of things of space; on the Sabbath we try to become attuned to holiness in time.
>
> ABRAHAM HESCHEL, *THE SABBATH*

We learned to slow way down. Relishing the silence, we got up slowly, ate leisurely breakfasts, went for long walks, read for hours at a time. Sometimes Dave took his binoculars to the field on the other side of the main road to watch birds. While he was out, I wrote long letters. Often we read the Bible together and prayed at length about various needs. No need to rush anything. After our son was born, we met a Scottish family in our neighborhood with a baby close to his age. Sometimes we walked to their apartment for a Saturday afternoon visit.

Occasionally we walked to the river, a mile from our apartment. There the Jewish sabbath was most visible to us, as whole families walked along the river path in their best clothes. Grandparents, parents and kids strolled together, exuding an air of abundance and relaxation.

As darkness fell on Saturday evening, we could hear the buses and trucks begin to rumble along the main road. With the noise came a sense of loss. This set-apart time, this time of quiet and peace, was ending. Sure, it would be nice to be able to run errands again, and I often felt a flicker of enthusiasm that the stores would open and I could buy milk or bread. But something about that quiet time with no options felt rich and full.

WE ARE NECESSARY; WE ARE SUPERFLUOUS

It took me years to be able to articulate the significance of what we experienced during the sabbath in Israel. I understand now that observing a sabbath enables us to encounter a significant yet paradoxical truth about God. C. S. Lewis expresses this paradox in his space novel *Perelandra*, where one of the angels says that we humans are both infinitely necessary and infinitely superfluous in God's eyes.

The first half of this paradox affirms that God wants us to serve as his hands and feet, stewarding the creation and making his love known in a world that needs it desperately. We who love God are indispensable; God depends on us to bring order to the world and reveal Christ's love. During the six days of the workweek, he asks us to faithfully fulfill this calling with hard work and perseverance.

Richard Lischer, professor at Duke Divinity School, describes the first half of this paradox: "When we do any kind of useful work, we join the act of creation in progress and help God keep the universe humming. . . . Farmers, construction workers, nurses, teachers, steelworkers, but most of all, those who perform acts of mercy toward their fellow human beings—all do the works of God that sustain the universe."

The other half of the paradox affirms that even though our work is valuable and necessary, even though God has created us to be his partners in sustaining the universe, he is fully capable of bringing about his purposes without us. We are creatures, completely dependent on the One who created us and sustains us. God alone is in control, and God alone upholds the universe. God's love alone preserves us and empowers us. We rest in that love, in that reality, on the day that we stop.

> It is obvious to me that the sabbath
>
> is part of the God-designed cycle
>
> we live in.
>
> BETH, A WOMAN IN HER FIFTIES

We also depend on God for salvation. "For by grace you have been saved through faith, and this is not your own doing; it is the gift of God—not the result of works, so that no one may boast" (Eph 2:8-9). When we work hard seven days a week with few breaks, we can subtly become convinced that we are earning salvation, that God's love and salvation come to us because we deserve it. The sabbath helps us know experientially that nothing we do will make God love us more.

The rhythm of six days of work and one day of rest enables us to experience profound truths about God and about ourselves—our necessity and our insignificance. If we stay in work mode all the time, or even if we rest all the time, our heart-based, experiential understanding of these truths will be flawed.

RETURN HOME

We returned to Seattle in 1980. About a month after we moved back home, we attended a conference where we met up with lots of old friends. Of course they asked about our time in the Middle East, and we described many aspects of our two years away. They were interested and receptive until we got onto the subject of the sabbath, at which point most people glazed over. They simply were not interested.

One friend, however, argued at length with us. Carl pointed us to Hebrews 4, which talks about our sabbath rest being fulfilled in Christ. There is no more need, he said, for God's people to observe a sabbath. He also talked about Colossians 2:16-17, where the apostle Paul says that we should not let anyone condemn us in matters of how we observe the sabbath, because it is just a shadow of things to come, and the substance belongs to Christ. He said the Pharisees in New Testament times were legalistic in their sabbath observance, and we needed to be careful not to fall into legalism.

His talk of legalism and condemnation felt completely antithetical to what we had experienced in Israel. Week after week we had received the gift of a day when we stopped because we had no other option. Week after week on the sabbath we had experienced a quality of resting in God that seemed wholly good, that brought only good fruits of obedience and love for God.

I knew I wanted to continue to experience the gift of the sabbath even though I couldn't explain why and even though our Christian friends didn't understand it. Dave and I decided we would continue to eliminate options one day a week, even if the American culture didn't eliminate them for us.

We decided on Sunday for our sabbath. We would begin with worship at church, and then we would do the kinds of things we did in Israel: walk, read, play with our son, get together with friends. My husband was teaching again at the University of Washington, and he decided not to prepare for classes on Sunday. We would do house projects, repairs and errands on Saturday in order to keep Sunday free from work. We would refrain from shopping on Sundays, both to limit our options and to help prevent others from having to work on Sundays.

After we returned from Israel, I stayed home with our children (one more son soon came along) and went to seminary part time, taking ten years to complete a three-year degree. During my years as a student, I didn't study on Sunday. I decided not to do housework, laundry, grocery shopping or any of the other tasks that go into making a home. I did cook, however, so we could have friends over for meals.

> The truth must be told: With all the money in the world, and no time, we have nothing at all.
>
> WAYNE MULLER, *SABBATH*

As we began our sabbath practice, we didn't know of anyone else doing the same thing, people who could have helped us. We didn't know about many rich sabbath practices we could have established. I wish we had instituted a family gathering on Saturday evening to start the sabbath, with candles to welcome it. I wish we had said a blessing to communicate our affirmation to our children as Jewish families do, and I wish we had ended the sabbath with another gathering to help us go joyfully into the week.

Still, despite my regrets, I remember wonderful Sundays when our kids were little. Long walks with the boys in strollers. Bike rides with the kids on the back or, later on, riding their own adorable miniature bikes. Throwing bread to the ducks and geese at the lake near our house. Leisurely trips to the zoo. I remember reading aloud to the boys on rainy afternoons, times when I could relax and not worry about what I should be accomplishing around the house. I have fond memories of my husband watching the boys for an hour so I could take a walk by myself.

We felt completely alone in our sabbath practice. In the 1980s no one else seemed remotely interested in the concept. However, as the years went by, little flickers of interest appeared. Eugene Peterson wrote several significant magazine articles about the sabbath. Marva Dawn's book *Keeping the Sabbath Wholly* encouraged people to think about a day each week for ceasing, resting, embracing and feasting, and more people became interested in grabbing hold of this gift.

CHANGES TO THE PATTERN

After I graduated from seminary in 1990, I worked for seven years as a freelance writer, editor and teacher using a home office. So my sabbath pattern now involved one more discipline. I continued to cease from housework, but I also stayed out of my office. I didn't turn on the computer, look at mail, prepare for classes I was going to teach or engage in anything connected with my paid or volunteer work.

In 1990 our boys were eight and ten, and around that time our sabbath practice began to change in subtle ways. While we continued to attend church as a family, the boys began to have their own desires for Sunday afternoons, particularly involving connections with their friends. We never fought that transition or insisted that Sunday was a family day; we let the day change with each life stage. As the boys became more engaged with their friends, Dave and I increasingly saw Sunday afternoons as a time to be together, just the two of us. If one or both of the boys wanted to do something with us, fine. If not, then we just relaxed together.

My sabbath changed again in 1997 when I was ordained as an associate pastor in a Presbyterian congregation. Now Sunday mornings felt like work. Often I was teaching, preaching or lead-

ing worship. Even if I had a Sunday free from up-front responsibilities, I usually touched base with a dozen individuals on Sunday
morning, checking on how they were doing personally, briefly discussing tasks and projects, sometimes praying with a congregation
member for a specific need.

Meanwhile, my husband's job had changed and he had Mondays off. Our boys were close to being out of the house and
only occasionally wanted to do anything with us on Sunday.
We decided on a new timing for our sabbath. It would begin at two o'clock on Sunday afternoon and last twenty-four
hours.

We benefit by being ready to take on the workweek without feeling like we were cheated out of a weekend by working the whole time.

KURT AND MAGGIE, A COUPLE IN THEIR FIFTIES

I found I needed time alone
on Sundays after the very people-intense mornings. So Dave
would often exercise alone or spend time with a friend or one of
our boys. On Sunday evenings we often got together with friends
or family for a relaxed dinner. Dave's and my sabbath time together
was Monday morning. We got up slowly and spent the morning
walking for an hour or two, choosing a place close to nature. We
ate lunch together at a restaurant and came home in the early
afternoon mellow and relaxed. Sometime in the late afternoon, I
began to get organized for the week, easing back into the workweek by doing some planning and organization.

At the beginning of 2001, three things happened within several
months, again causing us to change our sabbath pattern. Dave began having to work on Mondays. Our congregation added a Sunday evening service. Even though I didn't need to be there every

week, I had to attend often enough that I knew I couldn't start my sabbath on Sunday afternoon. And, to top it all off, I injured my knee and could no longer take the long walks that had been a part of our sabbath routine for many years.

For the first time, Dave and I began to have different sabbaths. His is all day Sunday, and mine is all day Monday. We've had to come up with new ways to spend time together as a couple, because for many years the sabbath was central to our marriage experience.

LOVED APART FROM WHAT I DO

My current Monday sabbath is the least consistent with biblical patterns of any I've observed. It is Monday, not a day mentioned in the Bible with any connection to the sabbath. I observe the sabbath almost completely alone, with no family rituals, no affirmation of relationships with people. I attend worship on Sunday, the day before my sabbath.

> I would make more money if I worked on Sunday. But I pay a personal cost for those dollars, and the tradeoff isn't worth it.
>
> ANGELA, A SELF-EMPLOYED WOMAN IN HER FORTIES

Yet these past few years of spending the sabbath alone have nurtured my friendship with God in new ways. My Monday sabbaths, despite their departure from patterns in the Bible, tell me deep inside, in some primordial way, that God loves me quite apart from what I do.

I have never liked housework or home repairs. Having a day each week free from those two things—for more than twenty years—has been a gift of grace. God seems to be saying through that gift, "I know these things are hard for you. I'll give you rest from them."

However, I love my church work and my writing. I feel that I'm using the gifts God gave me to make a contribution in the world. As I take a day off from what I love, God seems to say, "Sure you love what you do, but I want you to love me more. Let go of your need for competence, your need for completion, and rest. Enjoy being with me. Notice how good I am. Spend time looking around, and pay attention to my many gifts to you."

ADDICTION TO "DOING"

Recently I talked with Carl, the same friend who told us years ago that observing a sabbath is legalistic. Carl has worked in Christian ministry his whole life. But as he approaches retirement, he is discovering that he needs the sabbath and has begun setting aside one day each week for resting in God. He is experiencing a growing conviction that the sabbath commands in the Bible still apply today.

Carl notes that even though he has been a Christian since childhood and has striven to grow in Christ all those years, his faith has not delivered him from an addiction to "doing." He reflects, "Sabbath keeping is a spiritual discipline that enables me to hack away at that addiction, much as fasting for others is a discipline related to an eating addiction. Doing seems to be woven into the fabric of that which stamps us as human, but it can become an end in itself."

Carl now believes that the sabbath command comes from creation, not from Old Testament law. Genesis 2:2-3 tells us God rested after he created: "And on the seventh day, God finished the work that he had done, and he rested on the seventh day from all the work that he had done. So God blessed the seventh day and hallowed it, because on it God rested from all the work that he had done in creation." Carl says, "I cannot ignore the fact that God rested, and it doesn't appear to be a condescending act, like a parent talking baby talk to two-year-olds who will eventually grow out of that need."

Ultimately, Carl says, the sabbath keeps him from being dehumanized. We are human beings, yet we live as if we were "human doings." We move through our days as if what we do mattered more than who we are. The sabbath is an opportunity to reclaim our heritage as children of God, created by God to live in grace.

Like many people, Carl feels compelled to finish what he starts. For much of his adult life, he believed he would rest when he finished the task at hand. He says, "I have reluctantly come to the conclusion that work never ends. Sabbath is God's gracious 'five o'clock whistle' that gives me permission to stop and lay down my tools, ready or not. And in the laying down of the tools I hopefully gain a better ability to decide between needs and callings."

> If we refuse rest until we are finished, we will never rest until we die. Sabbath dissolves the artificial urgency of our days, because it liberates us from the need to be finished.
>
> WAYNE MULLER, *SABBATH*

QUESTIONS FOR REFLECTION, DISCUSSION AND JOURNALING

1. Reflect on the word *stop*. What emotions does that word evoke? If God were to ask you to stop something for twenty-four hours each week, what might it be?

2. Think back to a situation where you were forced to stop your

normal activities. What did you enjoy? What did you learn? What did you find difficult?

3. Can you identify in yourself any tendency toward addiction to doing? Have you ever engaged in habits that helped you address that addiction? What habits make the addiction stronger?

PRAYING ABOUT THE SABBATH

Spend some time praying about your reactions to stopping and about your tendencies to be addicted to doing. Ask God to speak to you about these areas of your life, and ask for a willing heart to listen to his voice and respond in obedience.

CHAPTER THREE

Does God Get Tired?

THE SABBATH IN SCRIPTURE AND CHRISTIAN HISTORY

You shall keep my sabbaths, for this is a sign between me and you throughout your generations, given in order that you may know that I, the LORD, sanctify you.

EXODUS 31:13

My friend was puzzled. "You say that the sabbath command comes from creation when God rested on the seventh day. Why would God need to rest? God doesn't get tired."

Good question, one of many raised by the Bible's teaching on the sabbath. The word *sabbath* is used in the Old Testament about one hundred times and in the New Testament about sixty. Three key passages from the early books of the Old Testament lay out the reasons for sabbath observance.

CREATION

In the beautiful and carefully composed poetry of Genesis 1, we read that God made the world in six days. On the first day he created light, on the second day the waters and on the third day the dry land. The pattern of light, waters and land repeats in the

fourth, fifth and sixth days. On the fourth day the lights are organized to mark day and night. On the fifth day the waters bring
forth living things, and on the sixth day the land brings forth creatures. So these six days of creation are divided into two sets of
three days.

The pattern changes on the seventh day:

> Thus the heavens and the earth were finished, and all their
> multitude. And on the seventh day God finished the work
> that he had done, and he rested on the seventh day from all
> the work that he had done. So God blessed the seventh day
> and hallowed it, because on it God rested from all the work
> that he had done in creation. (Gen 2:1-3)

The phrase *seventh day* is repeated three times, but this time the
threefold repetition occurs within one day, emphasizing that day's
significance. The word *sabbath* is not used in this passage, but
the two Hebrew words trans-lated as "rested" both come
from the same root as *sabbath*. That root means "cease, desist,
stop, pause or rest."

The creation theme is re-peated in the first version of the
Ten Commandments, found in Exodus:

The abundance that makes sabbath rest possible amply proves God's providential care. In the sabbath celebration of abundant life, holiness and blessing converge.

RICHARD LOWERY, *SABBATH AND JUBILEE*

> Remember the sabbath day, and keep it holy. Six days you
> shall labor and do all your work. But the seventh day is a sab-
> bath to the LORD your God; you shall not do any work—you,
> your son or your daughter, your male or female slave, your

livestock, or the alien resident in your towns. For in six days the LORD made heaven and earth, the sea, and all that is in them, but rested the seventh day; therefore the LORD blessed the sabbath day and consecrated it. (Ex 20:8-11)

This emphasis on the sabbath's origin at creation indicates that the sabbath was created for everyone, not just the Jews. All creatures, including slaves, resident aliens and animals, are invited into a weekly day of rest.

FREEDOM FROM SLAVERY

The emphasis changes in the second version of the Ten Commandments, found in Deuteronomy. Here the people of Israel are encouraged to remember that God freed them from slavery:

Observe the sabbath day and keep it holy, as the LORD your God commanded you. Six days you shall labor and do all your work. But the seventh day is a sabbath to the LORD your God; you shall not do any work—you, or your son or your daughter, or your male or female slave, or your ox or your donkey, or any of your livestock, or the resident alien in your towns, so that your male and female slave may rest as well as you. Remember that you were a slave in the land of Egypt, and the LORD your God brought you out from there with a mighty hand and an outstretched arm; therefore the LORD your God commanded you to keep the sabbath day. (Deut 5:12-15)

It was the exodus from Egypt, in which the Hebrews left slavery behind, that formed the nation of Israel, so this command is also rooted in creation—the creation of a nation. In contrast to the first sabbath command, this decree invites the people of Israel to remember the sabbath as something unique to them as God's chosen people.

The Old Testament attitude to the

sabbath was to regard it as . . .

a feast of the Lord, an opportunity

to concentrate in private and in public

on the things of God. Its atmosphere

was to be that of a joyful festival; its

observance to be taken very seriously

by all.

WILFRED STOTT, "SABBATH," IN THE *DICTIONARY OF NEW TESTAMENT THEOLOGY*

Jewish tradition emphasizes the difference between the words *remember* (used in the Exodus command) and *observe* (used in Deuteronomy). Rabbis teach that on Sunday, Monday and Tuesday we are to remember the preceding sabbath, experiencing joy while we look back at the lovely day of rest as a gift from God. On Wednesday through Friday we prepare ourselves to observe the next sabbath, looking ahead with joyful expectation. Thus the sabbath flows into the whole week, bringing its sweetness and fragrance to every day.

THE SABBATH IN PRACTICE

A day, in the Hebrew view, began and ended at sunset. So the Old Testament sabbath began at sunset Friday and ended at sunset Saturday. The foundational idea was to cease from work. The sabbath command to refrain from lighting a fire, which was used primarily for cooking, ensured that women, servants and slaves could enjoy a day of rest along with the men (Ex 35:3).

The sabbath was also to be a day of "holy convocation" (Lev 23:3), a day of celebration, feasts, festivities and joy. Specific sacrifices were commanded for the sabbath, along with the renewal of the Bread of the Presence in the tabernacle.

The sabbath rhythm marked the forty years the nation of Israel wandered in the desert. The people of Israel had left Egypt but had not yet arrived in their own land, and God provided food every day in the form of manna, which the Israelites gathered off the ground (Ex 16). Some gathered more, some gathered less, but each person had enough to eat for one day. When the people tried to store the manna overnight, it rotted and became full of worms.

However, supernatural intervention allowed a complete day of rest. God commanded the people not to gather manna on the sabbath. Whatever the people gathered on the sixth day proved to be enough for that day and the next. No worms grew in it, and it did not decay overnight.

Numbers 15 describes an incident in which a man was found gathering sticks on the sabbath. Moses and Aaron put the man in custody because they were not sure what to do with him. The Lord spoke to Moses, saying that the man should be put to death. Seminary professor Richard Lowery, in his book *Sabbath and Jubilee*, comments on this story:

> We're to depend on God and trust God to provide. While other nations worked seven days a week, Israel was to work six and trust God for the seventh.
>
> DOUG PAGITT, "THE CONSUMER TRAP," *LEADERSHIP JOURNAL*

It is understandable—though chilling to modern sensibilities—that the Bible sometimes treats sabbath violation as a capital crime. Violating sabbath is blasphemy because it attacks the very character of Yahweh as redeemer of Israel, the God who frees rather than enslaves, who offers lavish blessing rather than endless toil. Sabbath is a deep symbol of Israel's intimate relationship with God. Violating sabbath is like throwing your wedding ring in the face of your spouse or burning your national flag. It is a serious and public statement of a permanent rupture. Yahweh alone among the deities of the ancient world offers rest as the distinguishing mark of the covenant people. Violating sabbath signals the end of this unique relationship.

We know that the sabbath was observed during the seventh through ninth centuries before Christ because the prophets spoke out against violations of its spirit. Amos 8:4-6 describes how the people were eager for the sabbath to end so they could once again engage in commerce that trampled the poor. Part of the purpose of the sabbath for Israel was to practice justice as a redeemed people, so their behavior stood against the very heart of the sabbath. Jeremiah, Ezekiel and Isaiah also condemn laxity in sabbath observance.

LEARNING FROM THE SABBATH IN THE OLD TESTAMENT

The sabbath is a sign of God's invitation to rest because God is the creator and redeemer of his people. He rests at creation not because he is tired but because rest is a sign of completion and abundance. The universe is so well ordered, the creation so good, God's gifts to humanity so generous that God is able to rest.

We are invited to enter God's rest as an acknowledgment of his abundance; our rest indicates that we depend completely on the God who created and sustains us. That invitation holds true as much for Christians today as for Jews centuries ago. Our existence depends just as profoundly on God's creative and sustaining acts.

We are also invited to rest as a way of remembering that we are redeemed from slavery. In the Old Testament that redemption came in the form of release from bondage in Egypt. After Jesus' death and resurrection we continue to celebrate our freedom in Christ from slavery to sin, death and evil.

> Rest is security, political stability,
>
> a firm and benevolent grip on power
>
> to preserve life-giving order.
>
> Rest is shalom. God rests at the end of
>
> creation because God is able to rest.
>
> RICHARD LOWERY, *SABBATH AND JUBILEE*

Dorothy Bass notes that rooting the sabbath in freedom from slavery helps us remember the freedom God gives us in many areas of life:

> Slaves cannot skip a day of work, but free people can. Not all free people choose to do so, however; some of us remain glued to our computers and washing machines every day of the week. To keep sabbath is to exercise one's freedom, to declare oneself to be neither a tool to be employed—an employee—nor a beast to be burdened. To keep sabbath is also to remember one's freedom and to recall the One from whom that freedom came, the One from whom it still comes.

As we remember our freedom, we will naturally want to feast with joy and sing with exuberance as we acknowledge God our Redeemer, the one who sets us free from slavery.

This celebration of redemption calls us to exercise justice toward others who are enslaved in any way. That's why the prophets pronounced judgment on anyone who observed the sabbath for a day and the next day returned to behavior that exploited vulnerable people.

The Old Testament sabbath demonstrates the covenant relationship between God and his people. He had called them into a relationship that involved resting in his provision and reflecting his values in the world. The call was true in the Old Testament and continues for Christians today.

THE CENTURIES BEFORE CHRIST

In the three or four centuries before Christ was born, the sabbath became one of the defining characteristics of Judaism. The book of Nehemiah, one of the later Old Testament books, describes the strict sabbath observance that Nehemiah enforced as he led the people to rebuild Jerusalem after the exile in Babylon (Neh 13:15-22).

Self-defense was not permitted on the sabbath, and in 168 B.C., the Romans sacked Jerusalem because they knew they could succeed on a sabbath day. After that event, the rules about self-defense changed, but many other activities were forbidden. Jewish texts dating from around Jesus' time prohibited thirty-nine specific acts on the sabbath, including sowing, plowing, reaping, threshing, winnowing, grinding, sifting, kneading, baking, spinning, weaving, hunting, slaughtering, building, hammering and transporting.

When we keep the sabbath holy, we are practicing, for a day, the freedom that God intends for all people.

DOROTHY BASS, *RECEIVE THE DAY*

These prohibitions were designed to promote joy, celebration and feasting. The rabbis recommended worship, study of the Torah, warm family life and enjoyment of food as appropriate sabbath activities. The motive behind the prohibitions was to make room for celebration and relationships.

JESUS AND THE SABBATH

Jesus and his disciples observed the sabbath. Jesus' first public appearance, recorded in Luke 4, shows him reading from the scroll of Isaiah in the synagogue on the sabbath. Luke reports that it was Jesus' custom to be at the synagogue on the sabbath day.

Even during the six times Jesus clashed with the Jewish religious leaders over the sabbath, he did not dispute the significance of the sabbath day. Instead he focused on what is appropriate sabbath behavior, or to look at the bigger issue, the question of what the sabbath reflects about God to the people who observe it.

> When no one is working, it is hard to tell the difference between them by their achievements. They are equal as imagebearers of God.
>
> DON POSTEMA, *CATCH YOUR BREATH*

One of these disputes involved the disciples plucking ears of corn—forbidden on the sabbath—because they were hungry (Mt 12:1-8; cf. Mk 2:23-28; Lk 6:1-5). In replying to the Pharisees' accusations that his disciples had broken the law, Jesus cited the example of King David and his men, who ate forbidden food when they were hungry (1 Sam 21:1-6). Feasting, not hunger, was commanded for the sabbath. Jesus was pointing out an inherent contradiction in the Jewish sabbath laws of the time.

The other five sabbath conflicts between Jesus and the religious leaders centered around healings:

- the man with the withered hand (Mt 12:9-14; cf. Mk 3:1-5; Lk 6:6-10)
- the woman bowed down with infirmity (Lk 13:10-17)
- the man with dropsy (Lk 14:1-6)
- the man who had been infirm for thirty-eight years (Jn 5:1-17)
- the man born blind (Jn 9:1-41)

There was no real need for Jesus to perform these healings on the sabbath. None of the people was dying; none of them had an urgent medical condition. Jesus was teaching through his actions that the sabbath is a day of liberation, a day when people return to the joy of the world as God created it. The sabbath themes from the two versions of the Ten Commandments—creation and liberation—are present in Jesus' healings on the sabbath.

Jesus asks the Jewish religious leaders, "Is it lawful to do good or to do harm on the sabbath, to save life or to kill?" (Mk 3:4). He points out that Jewish law permitted people to take care of animals on the sabbath. How much more would God desire that a daughter of Abraham be set free from Satan's bondage (Lk 13:15-16)? Jesus questions the crowd: if an ox or a child fell into a well on the sabbath, wouldn't they pull that child or ox out? (Lk 14:5). God, he says, desires mercy and not sacrifice (Mt 12:7).

For Jesus, the sabbath was a day to do good, show mercy, save life and free people from bondage. These acts, appropriate for the sabbath, spoke of God's nature: a merciful God, the God who heals, the God who delivers people from evil. Acts that glorify God can never be a breach of the sabbath.

In Mark 2:27, in the argument with the Jewish religious leaders about his disciples picking grain, Jesus says, "The sabbath was made for humankind, and not humankind for the sabbath."

The sabbath is to be a gift, not something to which we slavishly conform. He seems to be implying that the thirty-nine sabbath rules of the time had stepped over a boundary. They had ceased being helpful and had become a burden.

In addition, in this passage Jesus establishes himself as the one who decides what behavior is appropriate on the sabbath. He concludes his comments to the Jewish leaders with a statement guaranteed to make them angry: "The Son of Man is lord of the sabbath" (Mt 12:8). Jesus' sense of his own authority seemed arrogant and audacious to the religious leaders of his time.

Again, Jesus was not disputing the importance of the sabbath. He wanted it to be a gift to God's people that communicated something significant about mercy and redemption. Still, his unwillingness to submit to every detail of the sabbath laws of the time had consequences in the early church.

THE EARLY YEARS OF THE CHRISTIAN FAITH

After the resurrection, Jewish Christians continued to observe the sabbath. In addition, they met on Sundays to celebrate the resurrection. As the gospel spread to Gentiles, serious questions arose. Did Gentile Christians need to obey Old Testament laws? The Jerusalem Council, described in Acts 15, dealt with this question. The sabbath was not mentioned, but the church's resoundingly clear conclusion indicated that Gentile Christians did not need to follow the Jewish law.

The apostle Paul, in his travels throughout the Roman world, continued to worship on the sabbath. He often spoke about Jesus in far-flung synagogues. He also met with Christians on Sundays to celebrate the Lord's Supper. Sunday gained a new name, "the Lord's Day." That title appears once in the New Testament (Rev

1:10) and more frequently in early Christian writings.

The sabbath is seldom mentioned in Acts and the New Testament letters. In Galatians, Paul argues passionately that Christians must not look to obedience to the law to earn God's approval. In Galatians 4:10, he condemns "observing special days, and months, and seasons, and years." In Colossians 2:16-17 he argues that Old Testament laws regarding food, festivals and sabbaths are only "a shadow of what is to come, but the substance belongs to Christ." The same point is made in Hebrews 4. The sabbath rest is fulfilled in Christ.

These infrequent mentions of the sabbath show how little the question of sabbath observance occupied the early church. Paul's letters and the book of Hebrews condemn observance of the law as a way to earn God's favor, and all the sabbath enthusiasts I know would agree with that point. All of them would also agree that the sabbath points to the rest we have in Christ.

I want to view the sabbath as the

beginning of the week, so that I enter

into my workdays with a spirit of rest

that carries over from the sabbath.

TOM, A MINISTER IN HIS FORTIES

In the early centuries after Jesus' resurrection, theologians concerned themselves with sorting out the ways in which the Christian faith differed from Judaism. Today we ask what Christians can learn from the Jews, but that question was simply unheard of in the early years of the church. When theologians did address the question of the Lord's Day, they focused on how it differed from the Jewish sabbath. Early Christians emphasized the Lord's Supper, prayer and meals together in the community as distinctive activities of the Lord's Day.

Still, rest was needed. In A.D. 321 Constantine, the first Christian emperor, declared Sunday a day of rest. He ordered that public works cease and law courts close, but agricultural work was excepted.

From that point on in Christian history we find an increasing commitment to Sunday rest, but theologians placed the greatest emphasis on freedom to attend worship. Sunday as the "Christian sabbath" is not found in any literature until the twelfth century, and even then it was not a common way to describe the Lord's Day. The early Reformers, such as Luther and Calvin, insisted on the value of Sunday as a day of rest and worship, but they did not regard Sunday as the Christian fulfillment of the sabbath. In fact, many Reformers stressed that Christians should worship God every day.

RECENT HISTORY

After the Reformation, a small number of Christians came to believe that the fourth commandment had been neglected throughout Christian history. These groups grew into the Seventh Day Adventists and Seventh Day Baptists, who believe that the Old Testament sabbath laws apply to Christians. These groups, a small minority of Christians, still observe a Saturday sabbath today.

In the centuries after the Reformation, most Christians on the European continent developed a relaxed approach to the Lord's Day. In Geneva, John Calvin enjoyed lawn bowling on Sunday afternoons after worship. In contrast, English and Scottish Christians had more interest in careful legislation of what should and shouldn't be done on Sundays.

Much of the motivation for strict rules in England and Scotland came from the fact that many people used their time off from work on Sundays to gamble, drink excessively and attend bawdy plays in theaters. British Christians established rules for appropriate Sunday behavior as a reaction to these immoral activities.

The English Puritans carried this desire to legislate Sunday activities the furthest. In the seventeenth century some of the most devout and law-oriented Puritans immigrated to the United States. Many were motivated by a sincere devotion to Jesus Christ, but their rigid Sunday rules made the Jewish leaders of Jesus' time look relaxed. In certain towns, people were forbidden to smile on Sundays and mothers were not allowed to kiss their children. Some towns appointed individuals to pay surprise Sunday visits to the homes of congregation members to see if any violations were taking place.

The Puritans' rigidity from two and three centuries ago affected life in the United States for a long time. Strict sabbath observance was not unusual in the late 1800s and early 1900s. However, by the middle of the twentieth century, things were starting to change, and in the second half of the twentieth century, most restrictions that gave us a weekly rhythm were gradually abandoned. And, of course, by 2000 the phrase 24-7 had come into common usage, showing a significant change in the way most people viewed the week.

An Approach for Christians in the Twenty-First Century

Throughout history, the Holy Spirit has worked in the church to bring about the kingdom of God in the world. As Christians we can expect to learn and experience new things because the Spirit brings us the living water of Jesus Christ. I believe the Holy Spirit is working now to motivate Christians to reconsider the connection between the Lord's Day and the Old Testament sabbath. Because our need for rest has become so urgent, Christians have begun to ask, "What can we learn from the Jewish sabbath? How can we reclaim a heritage that has been lost in many ways in the church?"

The Reformers understood the need for true worship every day of life. They emphasized the Lord's Day as a day for authentic and participatory corporate worship, with the goal of teaching people to bring their lives to God in daily surrender and praise. Their emphasis was necessary for their time and immensely helpful to all Christians who came after them.

We still need to participate regularly in corporate worship that engages the heart and mind. And we need rest. Worship with others on the Lord's Day, and rest on the sabbath: sometimes we get to experience these two days together, and sometimes they need to be separated. But we need both.

When my husband and I returned from Israel in 1980, we couldn't find a single Christian interested in discussing the significance of the Jewish sabbath. In the first decade of our sabbath observance, a couple of books on sabbath keeping were published. In the 1990s more books and articles were published, and I began to hear Christians talk about what a sabbath might look like. As I did the research for this book, I was stunned by the number of Christians who were observing a sabbath in one form or another. I believe this comes from the Holy Spirit's work in the church to call us back to this gift from God, the gift of rhythms in time, the gift of a day to rest in the reality that God is in charge of the universe and we are not.

The time is right to learn about rest from the long Jewish sabbath tradition. The need is great. The frantic pace, the exhaustion that accompanies it and the resulting emptiness call us back to a rhythm that includes stopping and resting. We are drawn to the words of Jesus about abundant life and his peace that passes understanding, but often we don't know how to access them. The sabbath is a concrete way to start, a practical and ancient solution to an enduring human need.

QUESTIONS FOR REFLECTION, DISCUSSION AND JOURNALING

1. What changes have you noticed during your lifetime in the weekly rhythm of the communities where you have lived? What are the positive and negative aspects of those changes?

2. When you read about Jesus' conflicts with Jewish religious leaders about the sabbath, what questions come to mind?

3. If you are not currently observing the sabbath, do you know people who are? What attracts you? What questions do you have? If you do observe the sabbath, what have you learned from it? What questions do you have?

PRAYING ABOUT THE SABBATH

Pray about the questions raised in your mind about the sabbath. Ask God for wisdom to move forward.

CHAPTER FOUR

A Day Without a "To Do" List

Be still, and know that I am God!

I am exalted among the nations,

I am exalted in the earth.

PSALM 46:10

W hat do you need to cease from?" Whenever I talk with an individual or a group about sabbath keeping, I ask that question.

"Rushing around and being busy all the time" is the most common answer. The second most common answer: "Multitasking, always trying to do more than one thing at a time."

The sabbath gives us a delightful opportunity to consider where we need to slow down, where our lives have too much motion and activity. Once we have decided when to observe a sabbath, we need to address two practical questions:

• On my sabbath, what will I cease from doing?

• What will I do during sabbath time?

In this chapter we will look at options for ceasing, and in the next chapter we will consider possibilities for what to do.

I have been observing a sabbath for twenty-five years, but I have never followed all the practices presented in this chapter. Neither should you. As we look at the possibilities, pick one or two activities to eliminate from your sabbath day. Cease from doing those things on the sabbath for three to six months. One or two weeks is not enough. See how it feels over time. Then perhaps try something else.

What are we invited to cease from doing on the sabbath?

CEASE FROM WORK

First and foremost, the sabbath calls us to cease from work. When God spoke the Ten Commandments to Moses, he said, "Six days you shall labor and do all your work. But the seventh day is a sabbath to the LORD your God; you shall not do any work—you, your son or your daughter, your male or female slave, your livestock, or the alien resident in your towns" (Ex 20:9-10).

Marva Dawn says simply, "The sabbath is a day to abstain totally from whatever is our work at the time." Do you work for pay? If so, then stopping any job activities on your sabbath is a good place to start. However, "work" goes far beyond what we do for pay. I began observing a sabbath while I was a homemaker, and for me housework, most shopping and gardening are work. Paying bills and managing money feel like work. I try to exercise diligently almost every day. Exercise feels like work.

Several of my close friends love to garden and shop. One of my husband's greatest joys is physical activity. They would undoubtedly include different activities on their list of work to avoid on the sabbath.

Homemakers, retirees, students and people who are unemployed, disabled or ill may find it challenging to figure out what constitutes their work. But remember, almost all humans work in one form or another. As you consider what work is for you, think as broadly as you can.

Several people told me they cease from doing anything on the sabbath that could appear on a "to do" list. That criterion works well to help them discern what constitutes work. One woman refrains from paid work and "anything that doesn't feel peaceful." The word *peaceful* is a guide to show her which sabbath activities are healthy.

A youth pastor told me his sabbath guideline: to stop doing things that he would later judge based on progress or production. Another man avoids anything that feels like work or an "accomplishment."

> Rest on the Sabbath as if all your work were done.... Rest even from the thought of labor.
>
> ABRAHAM HESCHEL, *THE SABBATH*

A school librarian ceases from all work unless it is something she really enjoys doing. She loves to read, so she often brings home new books from the library to read on Sunday, her sabbath. But on Sundays she doesn't do anything else related to her job.

Several university students told me they refrain from studying on Sunday. One student said, "I consider the sabbath to be a guilt-free 'no homework' day."

A research scientist in his thirties said, "I started keeping the sabbath when I was in college. From sundown Saturday to sundown Sunday, I avoided doing any schoolwork. This was difficult in spring because crew racing season had me tied up most of Saturday, and the workload at Harvard was unbelievable. But God honored

my keeping of the sabbath, and I found I could work more productively when rested. Through various remodeling projects, babies
and career changes, I have continued to keep the sabbath."

Mothers and fathers with young children face an additional
challenge because the work of parenting never stops. They may
want to arrange baby-sitting occasionally in order to have a special
day of rest on the sabbath. For a healthy week-in, week-out sabbath pattern, parents can choose to cease from the work associated
with parenting—tidying up, cooking, doing laundry, running
errands—and focus on enjoying their children without having to
worry about getting other things done.

WHAT I CEASE FROM DOING ON THE SABBATH

On my Monday sabbaths I do exactly what Marva Dawn suggests.
I avoid the work that is mine at the time. On Mondays I do almost
nothing related to my paid or unpaid work. I seldom turn on my
computer, even to write an e-mail to a friend, because the computer is such a large part of my workweek. Sometimes I answer the
phone, but I often let the answering machine pick up because the
phone is also associated with my work.

As I have asked myself what I need to cease from, I have come
to realize that my workweek is dominated by generating words.
Words I speak on the phone, in meetings and in public. Words I
speak to God in intercessory prayers for people. Words I write on
the computer in e-mails, church newsletter articles, handouts for
classes I teach at church, articles for magazines, chapters for
books.

On the sabbath I need freedom from producing words, both
spoken and written. My current Monday sabbaths, spent alone,
help meet that need. I take time to notice the beauty of the world

around me, thanking God in a wordless way for the wonder of his gifts to us. I spend time reflecting on my life without the need to put anything into words.

Sometimes I sit on the living room sofa and look at the trees outside the window. I take the time to savor the experience in the moment—perhaps the greatest luxury life can give—but I don't put pressure on myself to articulate. I just experience.

A friend often spends a day at her cabin, where she reads, sleeps, thinks and journals. She says, "The most beneficial thing on that day is for me to have time to slowly reflect as my mind and heart drift." That's exactly what I do on Mondays. I let my mind and heart drift.

I do, however, discipline the direction my heart and mind take. I don't think about what I have to do that week. If an upcoming task comes to mind, I gently set it aside. If I'm particularly anxious about remembering something I need to do, I'll get out my calendar and make a note, then try to forget about it until Tuesday.

On my sabbath I try not to think about unfulfilled desires. I don't let my mind go for long in the direction of material possessions or things I don't like about myself. I try to keep my thoughts free of kitchen remodels and car repairs, cellulite and diets. I focus on the present, noticing the beauty of God's world, or the past, dwelling on how God was present in a specific event. I don't spend time nurturing regrets or disappointments.

Over the years I have experimented with ceasing from different things, and I have made changes from time to time. When I first started keeping a sabbath, I allowed myself to cook so we could have company for dinner. Then for about ten years I tried not to cook on Sunday, making an effort to prepare a casserole or large batch of soup on Saturday.

In the past few years I have cooked more on my sabbath, trying to do it slowly and intentionally, enjoying the smells and the tastes, noticing the color of the vegetables, feeling the warmth from the pan, letting my thoughts wander as I stir. On weekdays when I cook, I'm usually trying to get something else done at the same time, but on the sabbath, I simply focus on cooking.

FREEDOM FROM MULTITASKING

One of the greatest sources of stress in our world today is multitasking. Stress-related disease can be directly attributed to our drive to get many things done at the same time. One of the greatest gifts we can give ourselves is a day each week free from this compulsion to multitask.

Freedom from multitasking will look different for each person, but it may mean turning off cell phones while driving or keeping the computer off all day so we are not tempted to check e-mail while doing something else. It may mean talking to family members with undivided attention, listening to music with our eyes closed, driving to church without the radio on, or washing dishes without the TV. Each of us can look over the pattern of our lives to identify when and where we tend to multitask. Then we can choose to let go of those activities, just for one day, and the stress that goes along with them.

Freedom from multitasking is a breath of fresh air for people

On the sabbath we try to avoid any activity that creates a sense of hurry or stress. If that type of pressure exists, it doesn't feel like we had a sabbath at all.

TONY AND SARA, A COUPLE IN THEIR FORTIES

in any life stage, but particularly for busy parents. It feels wonderful to play with young children without the need to get anything else done. However, parents of school-age children often tell me they can't possibly keep a sabbath because their children have sports activities virtually every day. If this is the case for you, there are still options.

Some parents choose one day each week when their kids simply don't participate in sports. Others allow sports activities in a different spirit on the sabbath by refusing to multitask. No errands on the way to or from the game. No PDAs or laptops at the game. No talking on the cell phone or reading papers from work between innings. On the sabbath, parents can focus on enjoying the game and help their children do the same by reducing the emphasis on competition and winning. The sabbath is a perfect day to celebrate camaraderie with teammates, the joy of using our bodies and the rewards of sportsmanship.

In our time, multitasking is a significant part of most kinds of work, both what we do for pay and what we do to manage households and families. Allowing ourselves a day each week to focus on one thing at a time can be a wonderful gift from God.

FREEDOM FROM TECHNOLOGY AND MACHINES

We can also observe the sabbath by picking one heavily used appliance and letting it rest. This might be the washing machine, the dishwasher, the television, the computer or the car.

One woman in her twenties doesn't answer her phone on the sabbath and refuses to check her messages. On weekdays, retrieving messages and returning calls feels relentless, so she gives herself a break on the sabbath. In the same way, many people choose not to look at their e-mail on the sabbath, desiring a rest from the responsibility and sheer work of keeping up with their in-boxes.

A family with children in elementary and middle school observes "no-screen" Sundays. They shut off computers and video games on Sundays, as well as the TV. The kids have easily found other things to do on Sundays, but the parents report that they've had a harder adjustment, finding it challenging to go all day without checking e-mail.

Technology has an enticing aspect to it, drawing us into the materialism and competition of our culture. Video games promote a "win at all costs" agenda. The Internet puts information at our fingertips and allows us to order products with the touch of a button. Taking a day off from that competitiveness and acquisition can provide a helpful rest. In addition, turning off the television, video game or computer makes space for relational connections and combats technology's isolating tendencies.

> If an activity feels like something
>
> I "have to do," I try to do it on other
>
> days. If an activity feels like
>
> something I "get to do," then it's a
>
> candidate for the sabbath.
>
> DONNA, A WOMAN IN HER FORTIES

In one Jewish tradition, a box is set by the front door on Friday evening when the sabbath begins. Family members put into the box the various things they will not be using for the next twenty-four hours. In our day, the sabbath box might receive our car keys, watches, cell phones, laptops and remote controls. Closing the lid on the box reminds us that this is a time set apart from daily life.

Freedom from Media

Many people stop engaging with one or more forms of media on the sabbath. Television commercials encourage consumption and materialism, which seem opposed to the peaceful rest God wants to give us. Even magazines and newspapers, with their plethora of advertisements, can draw us into thoughts and desires we would do better to avoid.

One man doesn't read the Sunday newspapers because of the underwear ads. On the other six days he reads the paper to keep up with the news. As he turns the pages and stumbles upon pictures of mostly naked women in full-page ads, he struggles with lustful thoughts. He doesn't like to have to work that hard to fight his desires, so on Sunday he gives himself a break.

A couple in their thirties carefully screens the movies they watch on Sunday. They ask themselves if a movie could be called "holy" before they watch it on their sabbath, and many (perhaps most!) popular films don't make the cut.

In addition to considering the way media creates lust or draws us away from holiness, we can ask other questions: Do certain kinds of media exercise a form of mind control in my life, and do I need a day free from that influence? Do certain types of media draw me too far into our secular culture, and would I profit from a day to stand apart? Do some media create white noise that stops me from listening to God?

Freedom from Shopping

Linda, fifty-two, was raised in a family and church environment that observed the sabbath strictly. On Sundays her family took leisurely drives, played board games and invited people over for meals. No one could play sports or go shopping.

Linda has not consciously kept a sabbath in her adult life. However, she has chosen not to shop on Sundays because of something that happened when her children were very young. In those years her husband would watch the children on Sunday afternoons and she would go shopping as a way to get out of the house.

She reflects, "During those years when I shopped on Sunday afternoons, I found myself becoming greedy. I wanted things I didn't have, things that had never enticed me before. I observed that I was becoming a consumer. So I stopped shopping on Sundays, and I have never resumed. I am more content with what I have when I keep one day each week free from shopping."

In Jewish tradition the sabbath is a day to refrain from handling money, managing money and thinking about money. In our world, perhaps the best way to stand aside from money is to refrain from shopping. As many contemporary sabbath observers have found, this helps us step back from materialism and stand apart from our culture's emphasis on more possessions as the route to happiness.

Wayne Muller in his book *Sabbath* writes:

Sabbath is a time to stop, to refrain from being seduced by our desires. To stop working, stop making money, stop spending money. See what you have. Look around. Listen to your life. Do you really need more than this? Spend a day with your family. Instead of buying the new coffee maker, make coffee in the old one and sit with your spouse on the couch, hang out—do what they do in the picture [in the advertisement] without paying for it. Just stop. That is, after all, what they are selling in the picture: people who have stopped. You cannot buy stopped. You simply have to stop.

We crave things. We can try to quench that craving by purchasing. Or, Muller says, we can quench that thirst with sabbath tranquility. We can rejoice in what we already have. We can focus on our abundance rather than our lack. As we grow in our ability to rest in the abundance that is already ours, our hunger and thirst will fall away. And as those cravings fade in quiet stillness, we will be better able to identify our genuine needs and contrast them more clearly with our thoughtless wants and desires.

Ceasing from shopping can help us make space for many good things. It also makes fewer demands on the people who work in stores. In the sabbath law given in Exodus 20, God commands that entire families, their servants and their animals rest one day each week.

In our world few people have servants, but we do receive servant like help from people who wait on us in stores and restaurants. Many sabbath observers refrain from shopping and eating out on their day of rest so no one will have to wait on them. In my ideal world, so many people would stop shopping on Sundays that stores would close, shopkeepers and clerks would be with their families and friends, and we would return to a world where everything stops one day each week.

Freedom from Competition

Video games and other media can fire up a competitive streak. Sports can also do it. For people who engage in competition during their workweek, stepping aside from it on the sabbath can be rejuvenating.

Eric Liddell during the 1912 Olympics refused to run in a heat held on Sunday. Early in the movie *Chariots of Fire*, Liddell chides a group of young boys playing soccer on Sunday. A long history in Christian tradition invites us to consider avoiding competition on the sabbath.

As we become a culture in which our leisure activities define us as much as our work, we need to consider the competition inherent in many hobbies. Do I enjoy quilting because I love fabrics or want to please someone by making them a quilt, or am I trying to show I can make better quilts than my friends? Am I gardening to enjoy God's beautiful creation or to impress the neighbors? Do I participate in the adult softball league because I enjoy using my body on a team with others, or am I trying to prove something? The sabbath is a day to let go of the spirit of competition we fall into so easily.

Even preparation for competition can feel like work on the sabbath, as one couple in their forties found. Tony and Sara enjoy long-distance bike rides, which are quite popular here in Seattle. Every summer thousands of people in the Pacific Northwest participate in two-day bike rides from Seattle to Portland, Oregon, and from Seattle to Vancouver, British Columbia. Tony and Sara decided last winter to prepare for the ride to Vancouver. They had made the trip some years earlier, and they knew they would need significant training to do it again.

Tony says, "We were going riding as often as we could, including Sundays, but we were having trouble finding enough time to go for long rides. In the middle of the night, in a bout of insomnia, we talked about it and decided that we would skip the ride this year because it felt like 'too much work.' Two days later, on a Sunday, we went for a good long ride and had fun together, and the only difference was that we didn't have a deadline or a sense of 'gotta' anymore. We were just doing it for fun."

FREEDOM FROM TALKING

Some people embrace silence on the sabbath, affirming the words of the psalmist, "Be still, and know that I am God" (Ps 46:10). They might do this by observing an hour of silence on Sundays, either before or after church, or by driving to church in silence.

One man decided to stop talking altogether on Sunday. He looked at his life and realized his words were becoming cheap; his weekdays were filled with masses of words. When he first stopped talking on the sabbath, he and his family (not surprisingly) found it very difficult. After a while everyone adjusted, and he began to look forward to Sundays, when he could pursue his thoughts without discussing them with anyone.

For most people the sabbath provides an opportunity for relaxed relationships without pressure to accomplish tasks, so to cease from talking all day would be counterproductive. However, we can learn something significant from this man who examined his life to discern what was becoming cheap. What activity in your life has lost its value because of overuse? What is in danger of losing its value? It could be something as pleasant and life-giving as gardening or something routine like driving, talking on the phone or using the Internet. Whatever it is, it may be a candidate for elimination on the sabbath so that its value may be restored to you.

FREEDOM FROM ANXIETY

If shopping arouses desires for possessions and sports bring competitive attitudes to the forefront, what activities raise fearful thoughts and anxious feelings? For those of us whose thoughts easily move toward fear, we can experience God's peace by keeping a day each week free from slavery to anxiety.

On the sabbath I try to stop worrying or

being anxious about the things that

occupy my life during the week.

JESSIE, A STUDENT IN HER EARLY TWENTIES

Marie, twenty-five, an administrator for the state, calls herself a "worrier" and has tried many times to stop fretting so much. One of her friends talked with her about the psychological benefit of the sabbath. Our bodies need a break from worry and stress, this friend said. Marie liked the idea of attempting not to worry one day each week; that seemed manageable to her. While she acknowledges that she doesn't always keep from worrying, she says, "The overarching theme for the sabbath is not doing things that worry or stress me."

Dorothy Bass, in her book *Receiving the Day*, recognizes that for those of us who tend to worry, the more we try not to think of something, the more it intrudes into our thoughts. However, she says, we can structure our sabbath day to make worry less likely.

We can refrain from activities that we know will summon worry, activities like paying bills, doing tax returns, and making lists of things to do in the coming week. On Sundays, one wise woman deliberately refrains from thinking about people who make her angry, practicing letting go of the slights and grudges that accumulate over the course of any week. And we can cultivate those forms of engagement with nature, ideas, and other people that really get our minds off of the week ahead. For my son, that means shooting hoops with a friend, and for me, watching him do so.

Closely related to worry is the kind of negative self-talk that comes so easily to some of us. I have always disliked my body, and

I used to think I was alone in those feelings. In recent years as I have listened to other women talk about how they look, I have been stunned to realize I've never met another woman who likes her body.

A fitting sabbath discipline might be to try to cease from criticizing our bodies. To follow Dorothy Bass's suggestions, we can create structures that prevent us from focusing on our physical appearance. For me, that includes refraining from shopping for clothes or trying on outfits, abstaining from novels with beautiful and slim heroines, and refusing to overeat, which always sets up a cycle of self-disgust in me.

> What do I cease from on the sabbath?
>
> All that keeps me from reflection, wonder, finding joy in God, finding joy in God's creation, and finding joy in his people.
>
> CARL, A MAN IN HIS EARLY SIXTIES

DECIDING WHAT TO CEASE FROM

The reason given in Deuteronomy 5:15 for keeping the sabbath is that our ancestors were slaves in Egypt and went four hundred years without a vacation. What form of slavery do you fall into most easily? Slavery to criticizing your body, as I do? slavery to possessions? slavery to fear? to anger? to perfectionism? to finishing things?

We are invited on the sabbath to remember that we have been freed from slavery by the death and resurrection of Jesus. "For freedom Christ has set us free" (Gal 5:1). As we consider what we will cease doing on the sabbath, we will benefit most from choosing to refrain from activities that nudge us into slavery.

We have looked at many possibilities for ceasing on the sabbath: various kinds of work, multitasking, media, technology, shopping, competition, overuse, fears and negative self-talk. Pick a couple to eliminate on your sabbath. Try your new discipline in a gentle way for three to six months. Remember, one or two times is not enough. After your months of experimentation, spend some time reflecting on what has happened in your emotions and soul. See what you are learning about God. Watch for the impact on your family and friends.

I've learned how much control I want in my life. However, I've learned that even the little ways I try to observe the sabbath do help me draw nearer to the Lord.

CLAUDIA, A WOMAN HER FORTIES

Then talk with someone about your response. Perhaps you will want to make changes, vary the pattern slightly or start over with something completely new. Remember, we are striving to obey the spirit of the sabbath law. We are not trying to make rules or create new burdens. We are ceasing from some activities to make space for resting in God and enjoying the gifts he's given us.

QUESTIONS FOR REFLECTION, DISCUSSION AND JOURNALING

1. What do you need to cease from?

2. What is the role of multitasking in your life? In what ways is it exhilarating, challenging, addictive, exhausting or overwhelming?

3. What aspect of your life might be losing its value because of overuse?

4. When you think about ceasing from some of the activities described in this chapter, what fears come up? What might happen, both positive and negative?

PRAYING ABOUT THE SABBATH

Spend time praying about your reactions to this invitation to cease from certain things on the sabbath. Ask for God's guidance about what is best for you to cease from doing. Bring your fears to God.

CHAPTER FIVE

The Making of a Sabbath Celebration

Thus says the LORD:

Stand at the crossroads, and look,

and ask for the ancient paths,

where the good way lies; and walk in it,

and find rest for your souls.

JEREMIAH 6:16

One Sunday after church I ran into Anna and Erik and their two young children. We walked to our cars together.

As soon as I fell into step with them, Anna turned to me and said, "I have a sabbath question for you. I have this hobby that I haven't been able to do since I had children, and I'm thinking it would be a good thing to do on Sundays. I want to see what you think."

Anna is a very energetic woman in her midtwenties who teaches piano lessons and enjoys keeping a clean house. We had already had one conversation about the sabbath, in which she told me that Erik insisted she keep Sundays free of housework. He saw her tendency to try to be productive every minute and wanted her to experience rest, and she was grateful, most of the time, for his insistence on a day of rest.

She continued, "What I'd like to do on Sundays is a hobby I really love, something I used to do a lot, something I found relaxing and enjoyable."

I responded, "I certainly believe we should do things we find relaxing and enjoyable on the sabbath."

"It's scrapbooking," she announced. "I used to make special photo albums. I'd like to start doing it again."

I said, "As long as it stays relaxing, that's fine. As soon as it becomes work, or as soon as you absolutely need to get it done, then stop doing it on Sundays. Make sure it is a satisfying thing to do."

"What if it's satisfying because I'm getting it finished? I love to get things finished!" she said.

"Ah, but that's the danger," I reflected. "As soon as something becomes compulsive, as soon as we're doing it because we want to get it done, then we need to stop doing it on the sabbath."

"Then maybe I won't be able to do anything on Sundays!" she laughed.

"DOING" AND THE SABBATH

In this chapter we will look at what we can do on the sabbath to experience true rest and draw near to God. This includes ceremonies to mark the beginning and end of the sabbath and things to do in between. Most books on sabbath keeping present practical suggestions, and just about every experienced sabbath keeper has good ideas too. These next pages present a variety of suggestions.

However, I write these words with fear and trembling. If they create in you a sense of obligation, then I will have defeated the very purpose of the sabbath. If the various possibilities—worship services, candles, festive meals, prayers, walks, special games and so on—become one more way to be successful or productive, another burden to carry, then the spirit of the sabbath will be violated.

On the sabbath we are invited to clear away the distractions of our lives so we can rest in God and experience his grace in a new way. We may need to create some simple structures to experience true spiritual rest in God's presence. But if we give ourselves too many things to do, the sabbath becomes a legalistic and burdensome duty.

The sabbath is more than doing nothing all day. However, doing nothing of any particular importance on the sabbath has, over the course of many years, taught me more about God's grace than anything else in my life. So we need to seek a delicate balance in our sabbath observance: lots of rest and a few habits to nurture intimacy with God and others.

Sabbath . . . is a time for "useless" poetry and other arts; a time to appreciate a tree, your neighbor, and yourself without doing something to them; a time to praise God as an end in itself.

TILDEN EDWARDS, *SABBATH TIME*

As you read these suggestions for activities to do on the sabbath, pick one or two to start with—three at the most. Try them for three to six months, then perhaps try something else. Experiment lightly, being gentle with yourself. The sabbath is about resting in God; it is not about feeling obligated to do something more.

BEGINNING THE SABBATH: THE JEWISH TRADITION

In orthodox Jewish families, preparing for the sabbath begins a day or two in advance. All the meals for the twenty-four hour period must be planned, the groceries purchased and the food cooked. The house is cleaned, and most people bathe and dress in something special late on Friday afternoon or in the early evening.

As sunset arrives on Friday, two candles are lighted, sabbath prayers are recited, and the family gathers to eat a special meal. Challah bread, rich and braided, is a treat reserved for the sabbath. The children receive a blessing from their parents.

Married couples are encouraged to make love on Friday nights. Saturday is a leisurely day, perhaps involving attendance at the synagogue, a walk for the whole family, a lunch with relaxed conversation, and a nap. In some traditions, Jews are encouraged to pray only prayers of thankfulness on the sabbath. Even intercessory prayers are viewed as too much work. However, deeds of mercy and compassion are encouraged as fitting actions.

The sabbath is the highlight of the week for observant Jewish families. The candle lighting and blessing on Friday evening welcome a day considered to be Bride and Queen of the people, a day that functions like a loving spouse who brings inner delight and a beautiful ruler who gives order and peace.

When I hear the longings of people I know, I hear a deep desire for "inner delight" and "order and peace." These can be gifts of the sabbath for us as well as Jewish families.

Many Christians pick a few aspects of the Jewish sabbath tradition to adopt for themselves. Candles seem to be a universal symbol of God's presence, of Christ's light shining in the darkness. Just about everyone enjoys a special meal. A sunset-to-sunset sabbath has the advantage of beginning in the darkness, so candles and a celebratory meal can mark the sabbath's start.

One missionary family with older children sets aside a fat candle for the sabbath. When they begin their sabbath at sunset on Saturday night, they light the candle and keep it lit until sunset on Sunday night, extinguishing it only when they sleep. The presence of that lit candle reminds everyone that this time is special, set apart from the rest of the week.

A simple prayer or psalm can easily be used to mark the beginning of the sabbath, whatever time of day it starts. For those whose sabbath begins in the morning, a set-apart feeling can be created by waking up more slowly, eating a special breakfast, lingering over coffee, or spending a few moments watching the birds outside the window.

WORSHIP WITH OTHERS

Central to the Christian practice of the sabbath is worship with a community. For many Christians, attending a worship service is the only activity that marks the sabbath as a special day. Sunday afternoon the errands begin, the family scatters, and the pace of living never slows. Viewing a worship service as the sole expression of the Christian sabbath causes us to miss out on much more.

However, community worship does serve as a significant foundation for the sabbath. People who work on Sundays and observe a different sabbath day will need to pursue worship opportunities that fit their schedules. Perhaps they will worship on a different day from their sabbath, but in their minds they can connect the worship experience to the sabbath day.

Some people view worship attendance as an agonizing obligation, perhaps because of a history of damaged relationships or too many volunteer responsibilities. Maybe the worship itself is not satisfying or engaging. These painful situations require prayer and reflection to discern how to respond. Experiencing a distressing obligation every week on the sabbath prevents the kind of rest God designed for us.

WHAT I DO ON THE SABBATH

I attend corporate worship on Sunday morning, and I observe the sabbath on Monday. In my mind I connect Sunday worship to my Monday sabbath, because I want the sense of God's presence I experience in worship to overflow into my sabbath day. In one sense, a piece of my sabbath happens on Sunday morning and the rest of it happens on Monday.

As I have considered what to do on the sabbath, I have been strongly influenced by a Jewish sabbath prayer:

Days pass,
Years vanish,
And we walk sightless among miracles.

I have tried to embrace the sabbath challenge of figuring out what activities enable me to see the miracles of God more clearly.

I attempt to start the day in a way that differs from my normal morning routine. On the sabbath I wake up slowly and spend time lying in bed staring into space, luxuriating in the fact that I don't have to produce anything for a whole day. I try to engage my senses. I relish small sensations, like the feel of the sheets on my skin and the warmth of the cozy nest that has been created in my bed overnight. I open the blinds and observe the sky. If I can remember a dream, I take some time to think about what it might mean.

Before I get out of bed, I thank God—in a kind of wordless

way—for the beauty of this sensory information, for warmth and my skin's ability to feel, for the sky and my eye's ability to see, for anything I can smell. I think about what I will eat for breakfast, and I thank God for taste. As I lie in bed, I also thank God for the abundant blessings he has given me: family and friends, satisfying work to do, a comfortable place to live, food to eat, books to read, ideas to pursue, a body that mostly still works, and on and on. For me, engaging my senses helps me be thankful, and beginning the day with thankfulness sets the tone for a day of luxury, leisure and rest that will increase intimacy with God.

Can one reach God by toil?

He gives himself to the pure in heart.

He asks nothing but our attention.

WILLIAM BUTLER YEATS

I usually spend Mondays alone. Often I set aside a novel earlier in the week, and I read much of the day. Occasionally I go out for breakfast or lunch alone. I sew, listen to music, do a craft or spend hours reading the Sunday paper. Sometimes I shop for something frivolous—no running errands!—and try to enjoy the sights, sounds and smells as I shop. Whatever I do, I do it slowly with lots of breaks. I often stop reading and look out the window.

In fact, I try to spend the whole day attuned to beauty. Catholic theologian Leonard Doohan believes that "the ability to experience something beautiful prepares one for the beautiful experience of God." He believes that joy works in the same way. As we enjoy life, we are opening our heart to enjoy God's presence. On my sabbath I try to nurture joy and cultivate my ability to appreciate beauty, which feels lovely and life-giving in the short term, and in the long run helps me draw closer to God.

I love the ancient Christian prayer called *examen*, typically exercised in the evening, in which we look back over the day to see where God was present. *Examen* is a gentle, unforced noticing, with the goal of allowing God to bring to mind what he wants us to see. In *examen*, we don't have to strain over every detail of our schedule to find God; we just reflect back in a prayerful way.

At some point during the day I practice an informal kind of *examen* of the past week. I sit doing nothing, and while I am doing nothing, I let thoughts about the week surface. I gently review them, noticing where God was present and what he was doing.

The key components of my sabbath celebration are lots of silence for reflection and lots of time to focus my senses so I can experience beauty and be drawn into thankfulness. I spend my workweek focused on people, ideas and words. Sabbath abundance and freedom invite me to pay attention to trees, clouds, the smell of a flower, the touch of clothing on my skin—all gifts of God.

ENGAGING THE SENSES

Many people find that experiencing God's creation is an important part of a restful sabbath, whether that involves gardening, walking, riding a bike or sitting in a park. Feeling the fresh air and seeing the sky and clouds and landscape clears away internal clutter. Being in God's creation often slows us down, which enables us to notice beauty, which in turn creates thankfulness and an attitude of receptivity. Nature often helps us listen to God more easily, particularly when we let our minds drift a little bit.

We are invited on the sabbath to breathe deeply, to enjoy nature, to watch a flickering candle, as a means to access the part of our hearts where thankfulness and God's peace dwell. We can engage our senses doing just about anything. If I need to drive somewhere on the sabbath, I drive more slowly than usual, noticing trees, clouds, interesting architecture, and people walking or jogging on the sidewalk.

Wayne Muller suggests:

> If we are to deeply and fully integrate rest into the rhythm of our lives, we need a sense memory, a visceral bodily experience of what it feels like to be delightfully inactive. . . . On the Sabbath we smell spices, we bring flowers, we smell the bread in the oven, and we are transported, we recall feelings and insights we have known before, and we remember. When the Sabbath is done and we return to our labor, we carry the fragrance of rest in our bodies.
>
> The Sabbath prohibitions restrict those things that would impede our sensuality. Walk leisurely, don't drive; walk in the garden, don't answer the phone, turn off the television and the radio. Forget the CD and the computer. Quiet the insidious technology, and remember that we live in bodies that, through a feast of the senses, appreciate the beauty of the world. Walk under the stars and moon. Knock on the door, don't ring. Sing at the table. Eat, drink, touch, smell, and remember who you are.

Taking in the beauty of God's world through the five senses can help us grow in thankfulness, both for the world God made but also for who he made us to be: his children, his friends, his delightful creation, his loved ones redeemed from slavery through Jesus Christ.

Some people enjoy caring for God's creation on the sabbath. This might involve walking instead of driving, or gardening organically. Riding a bike or walking to church not only reduces our impact on the creation but also helps us slow down and enjoy the beauty of the world in community with others. Some people choose to prepare a festive sabbath meal using all organic food in order to rejoice, for one day anyway, in treading lightly on the earth.

BREATHING, LISTENING

Many writers recommend paying attention to breathing as a way to slow down our racing thoughts and restless bodies and find, once again, that our life belongs to and comes from God.

Physiologically, slowing down our breath slows down many bodily functions. Spiritually, focusing on our breathing connects us with deep truths about God. At creation, God breathed into humans the breath of life

> All moments are holy moments,
>
> and life itself is grace.
>
> FREDERICK BUECHNER

(Gen 2:7). Every breath we take comes from God. Right after his resurrection, Jesus breathed on his disciples and said, "Receive the Holy Spirit" (Jn 20:22). In the same way that we breathe air, we are invited to receive God's presence over and over in our lives.

The sabbath is an opportunity to breathe deeply. It is described in Exodus 23:12 as a time when we may "be refreshed" or "catch our breath." I know that when I stop to take a few deep breaths, I am more able to focus on the moment. I am able to pay attention to the beauty around me, and I am more honest about emotions I am experiencing. If you have never tried to slow down your breathing for a few moments, it may sound crazy to hear that taking a few deep breaths can nurture thankfulness. Try it; you may be surprised.

Deep, slow breathing also makes me more available to listen to

God, which is a wonderful blessing on the sabbath day. Noticing God's gifts reminds us that we live receptively; everything good in our lives comes from beyond ourselves, and we can receive good things only as a gift from God. Once we are in that thankful, receptive frame of mind, we are able to receive love and truth from God as well. We are able to listen.

For me, thankfulness and listening on the sabbath involve breathing deeply, noticing sensory information, or just sitting and doing nothing. Others find journal writing helpful. One man in his forties, who has worked in Christian ministry all his life, has been practicing a particular sabbath discipline for twenty-five years. For two hours he sits with pen and paper in hand, listening to God. When he hears something, he takes notes.

This man has followed a variety of spiritual disciplines over the years, but the two hours of listening with paper and pen has not changed. He reflects, "We have such ridiculous expectations of what we can achieve, we work doggedly and we punctuate all our work with forms of recreation that don't help us rest. That means we don't work well, and we don't rest well. Part of sabbath rest is learning dependency on God. It's the only form of dependency that works."

One couple, both of whom work in intense ministry jobs, observe a two-day sabbath every week. On Sundays they spend time together with their two young children. On Mondays they take turns being alone. The husband spends several hours in the morning reading the Bible, praying and journaling while the wife stays with the kids. In the afternoon the wife takes her turn to spend time with God, and the husband cares for the children. Their goal in their time apart is to listen to God, and for them journaling plays an important role in that process.

FOCUSING ON GOD

One of the biggest challenges in planning the sabbath involves "spiritual" activities such as Bible study, prayer, journaling and other disciplines. Some people enjoy saving up prayer requests during the week so they can spend time in intercessory prayer on the sabbath. Some enjoy having a particular Bible-study focus for the sabbath. However, other people participate in intercessory prayer and Bible study on weekdays, and they will benefit from something different on the sabbath.

Whatever we do on the sabbath, we need to consider what helps us "seek the LORD and his strength." The psalmist recommends, "Seek his presence continually. Remember the wonderful works he has done, his miracles, and the judgments he has uttered" (Ps 105:4-5). I don't want to "walk sightless among miracles." I want to remember the good things God has done.

Throughout the Old Testament the people of God are commanded to remember. The various festivals were opportunities to remember the miracles of God. Christians today are also to pray prayers of thankfulness rooted in our clear memory of God's deeds. Stanley Hauerwas and William Willimon write:

> Sabbath is much more than doing nothing. We are enjoined this day to remember, recall, recollect, and re-create. We are not simply to remember that we ought to keep the Sabbath, but we are to remember who God is—active and loving, resourceful beyond our actions and resources. We are to remember who we are—gifted, sustained and blessed beyond our striving and achieving.

Because our culture puts all its emphasis on the things we don't have—so we can purchase something to meet that "need"—we have no natural structures to encourage us to remember what God has done, except perhaps Christmas and Easter. The weekly sabbath can be a wonderful opportunity to stop and notice God's goodness to us, to remember who God is and what he has done.

PRAYING AND PLAYING

Appropriate sabbath activities don't only include things that are serious, meditative and connected to prayer. One of the joys of being outside on the sabbath is the flat-out fun of using our bodies and being in the fresh air, both of them created by God and given to us to enjoy. Part of the purpose of a festive meal with candles and delicious food is the simple pleasure of a good meal with people we love, reflections of God's bounty.

Don Postema describes the dual nature of what we are called to do on the sabbath.

> Good sabbath-keeping includes both praying and playing. Prayerful sabbaths without play or playful sabbaths without prayer are only half-sabbaths. Prayer without play can degenerate into a dutiful and cheerless religion. Play without prayer can become mind-numbing escape.

Much of what is considered "play" in our culture easily slides into "mind-numbing escape." Perhaps a short session with a video game or a quick Internet search can be fun, but all too easily technology draws us into a place where we can no longer experience thankfulness or listen to God. Figuring out appropriate sabbath activities involves examining what is truly "play" for us, the kinds of fun and recreation that don't crowd out prayer but nurture it.

When people talk to me about what they enjoy on the sabbath, they describe bike rides and board games and outings to parks.

They talk about skiing and gardening for hours and long walks with close friends. They discuss leisurely, candle-lit meals with stimulating conversation and laughter. They talk about relaxed recreation that feels open-ended and luxurious, that enables them to do the things I've mentioned—breathe deeply, engage their senses, enjoy nature—and experience joy and fun as gifts from God.

One of my friends loves a particular beach in Vancouver, British Columbia. She says that on Sunday afternoons the beach is full of people having a good time, flying kites and kicking soccer balls and throwing Frisbees to their dogs. For her, that beach paints a lively picture of sabbath joy. It speaks to her of a kind of rest that demonstrates our freedom from both "dutiful and cheerless religion" and also "mind-numbing escape," rest that we experience best outside having fun with people we love.

The sabbath commands in Exodus and Deuteronomy remind us that God created an abundant world and also liberated his people from slavery. In the light of that bounty and freedom, what can we do except celebrate? Good food, rousing music, laughter and playful activities can help us revel in God's overflowing abundance and the freedom he has given us in Christ.

MAKING A LIST OF ACCEPTABLE ACTIVITIES

We do have to make decisions about what we will do on the sabbath, and many people have questions about how to go about that process. In fact, often we desire specific guidance. Can we ride bikes on the sabbath? What about jogging? If I have committed not to shop on the sabbath, is it all right to buy cough syrup for a sick child? We long for an approved list, a way of being sure we are doing the right thing.

One rabbi reports that his congregation wanted specifics about what they should and shouldn't do on the sabbath. He used three questions to determine whether an activity was suitable.

1. Does it promote rest and/or relaxation?

2. Does it bring delight and enjoyment?

3. Does it give you a sense of holiness and sanctity? In other words, does it add to your sense of Sabbath?

Some appropriate and enjoyable sabbath activities will come from a "yes" answer to one question. The most lovely and renewing sabbath activities will enable us to answer "yes" to all three questions.

In our daily lives, we are continually forced to deal with numbers, facts, details, tasks to finish and schedules to keep. We need to resist the temptation to make the sabbath one more item to check off a list, one more task to accomplish or one more thing we can measure. Celeste Perrino Walker in her book *Making Sabbath Special* recommends a spirit of celebration on the sabbath, and she says, "Celebration is more an attitude and less a bunch of activities to do."

> I think the focus of the sabbath should be to rest in God's presence.
>
> For me that can mean doing a variety of activities with that focus in mind.
>
> ANDREA, A WOMAN IN HER TWENTIES

Those of us who appreciate concrete instructions and specific suggestions may find it frustrating to hear that the sabbath is about attitude rather than a list of activities. That is why I have found it helpful to hold onto the Jewish prayer about walking sightless among miracles. I ask myself, *What will help me see God's miracles more easily?* That question gives me something more concrete to use as I assess sabbath activities.

PREPARING FOR THE SABBATH

However, there is a part of the sabbath experience in which lists can be helpful: the time before the sabbath starts. True relaxation on the sabbath requires preparation, and lists of things to get done before the sabbath begins can be beneficial.

I loved Friday afternoons when we lived in Israel. I could feel the anticipation of the day of rest just around the corner. Most people got off work sometime between noon and two o'clock. The sabbath would start around six o'clock, and I could feel the flurry of preparation in that interval of time.

People in grocery stores were bustling around cheerfully. On the occasions when we were invited to someone's home for a sabbath dinner, I would go to a nearby florist—lots of bustling there, too—to buy flowers for the hostess. People walked quickly on the streets, knowing they had things to do before everything shut down at sunset. Friday afternoons felt pleasantly excited, full of anticipation. To me, they did not feel frantic or overwhelming. Somehow everyone communicated their expectation of the time of rest and family relaxation that was about to begin.

> Why can't we just fall into a sabbath
>
> day without forethought?
>
> If you do, you will soon discover why.
>
> You find yourself involved in many
>
> little works that eat away at the
>
> difference and rest of the day.
>
> TILDEN EDWARDS, *SABBATH TIME*

A basic list of what to get done before the sabbath starts would include shopping for food and tidying the house. Having food on hand makes the sabbath much more restful, and a tidy house (or even just a tidier house) communicates the order and peace that many of us long for.

The list might also include menu planning and even cooking ahead for the twenty-four-hour period. Some people set a lovely table or bring out other decorations. Others clean the house thoroughly. Some sabbath observers find it helpful to do the laundry right before the sabbath, so everyone has choices for what to wear. Many people bathe and put on clean clothes.

I try to look over my schedule for the week to come before my sabbath starts. Do I need to prepare in any way for the next week? make a phone call to confirm an appointment? find some papers? If so, I try to do it then, before the sabbath starts. When I am careful to make preparations for the following week, I find my sabbath more peaceful. I am able to rest more fully.

The "work" of the sabbath needs to happen before the sabbath starts, so everyone can experience true rest on the day itself. Preparation for an activity helps us experience the value of that activity. A weekly discipline of sabbath preparation can add to our understanding that rest matters to God, that rest teaches us about God's grace.

ENDING THE SABBATH: THE JEWISH TRADITION

Jewish families light two individual candles as the sabbath begins. These candles represent how they feel going into the sabbath: God is present but seems a bit separate because of the weeklong focus on accomplishing tasks. As the sabbath ends, the family lights a braided candle. After a day of resting in God, life is once again intertwined with God, and the braided candle symbolizes that reconnection and intimacy. It represents the desire upon reentering the workweek to experience that intertwined reality every day.

In orthodox Jewish families, the end of the sabbath is also marked with brief prayers and a glass of sweet wine to celebrate the sweetness of the sabbath. A box of spices is passed around for everyone to smell, symbolizing the desire to carry the aroma of sabbath peace and joy into the week.

In the book of Jeremiah, God encourages his people to look for the ancient path, the good way. "Walk in it," the Lord says, "and find rest for your souls" (Jer 6:16). As we consider healthy patterns for sabbath keeping, we need to experiment to discover the ancient paths and the good ways that will enable us to find rest for our souls. What we choose to do on the sabbath needs to bring us rest and life over time. The challenge is discernment, experimenting to find what works for us and the people we love, what helps us catch our breath and remember who we are as God's beloved.

QUESTIONS FOR REFLECTION, DISCUSSION AND JOURNALING

1. What enjoyable activities are you not able to do during the week? Getting out in nature, gardening, reading poetry, drawing, writing in your journal? Consider whether those activities might be candidates for sabbath activities that could enable you to experience resting in God.

2. What helps you see God's miracles? What helps you be thankful? What helps you listen to God?

3. What one or two things would be most helpful for you to get done before the sabbath starts? What kinds of preparation would create a restful sabbath atmosphere?

PRAYING ABOUT THE SABBATH

Spend time praying about what might be healthy and life-giving
for you to do on the sabbath, both ceremonies to begin and end
the sabbath, and activities to do in the middle. Ask God to guide
you.

CHAPTER SIX

Too Busy to Rest?

OBSTACLES TO KEEPING A SABBATH

For thus said the Lord GOD, the Holy One of Israel:

In returning and rest you shall be saved;

in quietness and in trust shall be your strength.

ISAIAH 30:15

Busy. Exhausted. Empty.

If you ask people how they are doing, the most common answer is "busy." If you ask a few more questions about how they are feeling, you will usually bump up against exhaustion. If you persevere in asking about what is going on inside, you may well find out that many people feel empty.

Constant activity hasn't satisfied us at the deepest level, yet we continue to race around, somehow believing that a fast pace will bring us health and life. Ironically, the very symptoms that indicate our need for a sabbath are also the forces that keep us from attempting to set aside a day for rest. Many people feel they are just too busy to take time for rest.

Jeanne, in her early forties, cut back on her work hours to stay at home most of the time with her two daughters, both in elementary school. When Jeanne reflects on why she and her family don't build a day of rest into their lives, she realizes that they can't imagine losing any part of their busy schedule. She observes, "Our current life requires seven days a week to get everything done."

During some seasons of the year, Saturdays are swallowed up by sports, leaving Sunday for chores, projects and errands. Jeanne believes that a day of rest would make everyone feel they had sacrificed something and lost flexibility and freedom. "Honestly," she reflects, "I know I'd be worried about heading into Monday without my 'decks cleared' of chores, groceries, meal-planning, etc., which is a lot of how I spend my Sunday afternoons after church."

God created the sabbath as a day of rest for us, and I think we need to honor that no matter how crazy our lives are.

MARGIE, A SINGLE MOM IN HER TWENTIES

Most veteran sabbath observers would respond to Jeanne by saying they have found they get more done over the course of a week by resting one day. But most would also say that they would joyfully continue to keep a sabbath even if they got less done each week. The blessings resulting from a sabbath go much deeper than overall productivity.

A father of two sons in elementary school says, "We need to dethrone the quintessentially American belief that more time equals more productivity. We say, 'I don't have enough time to get it all done.' But life is not about 'getting it all done.' Life is not about filling every moment. Life is about gift, embracing and receiving God's gifts. God may want us to be inefficient sometimes in order for us to receive his gifts more fully."

Our need to focus on "getting it all done" comes from many places, including our view of time. Understanding the biblical view of time can help us change our focus.

TWO ASPECTS OF TIME

A few years ago I was asked to speak on the stewardship of time. I've always been good at organizing my time, so I thought I would be able to give some practical and helpful pointers about time management. However, I wisely decided it would be a good idea to look briefly at the Bible before I sat down to make notes for the talk.

I was quite surprised at what I found. To the biblical writers, time has two aspects. First, the Bible affirms the forward movement of time, looking to the things God will do in the future. In the Old Testament the prophets anticipate the coming of the Messiah and the time when God will restore the fortunes of Israel. In the New Testament, Jesus says that "his hour" will come, the time of his death. He promises that he will come back at a time known only to his Father in heaven. The apostle Paul and others write about their joyous expectations of heaven. In the Bible, time has a component of progress and anticipation of the future, an expectation of fulfillment and completion that God will bring about at the right time.

> Our world today is not supportive of a day of rest. Everything is twenty-four/seven, get as much done as we can, never sit still, be productive.
>
> SANDRA, A WOMAN IN HER FORTIES

In addition, time in the Bible has a strong sense of rhythm. Each aspect of the rhythm is an opportunity to remember God's work and express thankfulness. The daily rhythm of sunrise, mealtimes and sunset provides opportunities to stop and thank God for creating the world and providing for his people. Waking as the sun rises and getting ready to sleep as the sun sets are repeated opportunities to stop twice daily and remember God's faithfulness. In biblical times, prayers associated with hand washing before meals allowed people to stop and remember God's provision. Saying grace at mealtimes and praying bedtime prayers with children are two habits based on daily rhythm that continue in our time.

The people of Israel understood that the weekly rhythm of six days of work followed by one day of rest originated with God and his creation. Each week the sabbath rest provided an invitation to remember God both as Creator and as the deliverer of the people from slavery in Egypt.

Over the course of a year the rhythm of holy days also helped the people remember God's acts. At Purim the people of Israel celebrated Esther's faithfulness. At Passover they remembered that God spared them in Egypt. At the Feast of Weeks, also called Pentecost, the people celebrated God's giving of the Law. Hanukkah centered around a miraculous provision of oil for the temple. Various harvest festivals celebrated the ongoing reality that God provides.

The rhythm of time—daily, weekly and yearly—provided a structure for stopping, thanking, rejoicing and feasting. People understood and experienced the rhythm of time as an opportunity to acknowledge God's acts of goodness, mercy and provision.

WE'VE LOST THE BEAT

We have almost completely lost this sense of rhythm. We have electric light, so sunrise and sunset have little impact on us. We eat meals alone or at our desks, removing the opportunity for stopping and relaxing with others, saying grace together, remembering that God provides our sustenance.

We have adopted the term "24-7," which reflects our enthusiasm for blurring daily and weekly rhythms. In my childhood the weekly rhythm was still strongly in place, with almost all stores closed on Sundays and with sporting events scheduled for weekdays and Saturdays only. I was visiting England with my family in 1986 when a law was passed to allow most stores to be open on Sundays. And when we visited New Zealand in 2001, many stores and restaurants displayed signs boasting "Seven Days." It took me a while to realize the signs meant that these shops were advertising something new: they were open every day of the week.

> We can work without stopping,
>
> faster and faster, electric lights
>
> making artificial day so the whole
>
> machine can labor without
>
> ceasing. But remember:
>
> No living thing lives like this.
>
> WAYNE MULLER, *SABBATH*

Our connection with yearly rhythms has also changed. We can eat off-season fruit and vegetables from faraway places. We can travel to warm spots in the winter or become "snowbirds" and spend the entire season in the south. We do celebrate Christmas, Easter and a national holiday or two, but often those holidays become an opportunity for materialism rather than a pattern to help us remember what God has done in human life.

The loss of the rhythm of time dehumanizes us. Without a pattern of work and rest, we become machines of production rather than joyful children of the God who created and redeemed us. Yes, our work is immensely important. We are called to labor faithfully in the situations in which God has placed us. However, when work dominates our time, when we forget how to stop and rest and celebrate, we lose an essential part of the human experience.

We have also lost an accurate understanding of the forward movement of time. In the Bible, time moves forward toward God's fulfillment of all things. In our world, we certainly understand that time moves forward, but our priority is to maximize each moment in order to be successful, to accomplish, to prove that we are okay and deserve to occupy our place on earth. For us, time's forward movement involves achievement in the kingdom of this world. In the Bible, time moves forward because God is bringing about his kingdom.

When we embrace the Bible's view, we learn to watch eagerly for what God is doing rather than to focus obsessively on what we are doing. In order to watch for God's work, we need to stop long enough to notice it. A rhythm allowing time for rest is essential to perceiving the forward movement of time toward God's fulfillment of all things.

PRODUCTIVITY

One pastor recounts a time he was talking about sabbath keeping in a sermon series. Someone in his congregation came up to him and said, "I tried doing sabbath last Sunday afternoon. I stopped working and just rested. It was one of the worst times of my life! For a day to be worthwhile, I have to do at least one productive thing."

When my husband or I have had a particularly productive day, we say, "I got a lot done today. I justified my existence on the face of the earth." Our joke reflects an unfortunate reality that both of us battle. We tend to feel worthwhile when we accomplish things.

Part of why we choose to keep a sabbath is to fight all the messages from our culture and family backgrounds that reinforce our innate tendency to justify ourselves. We want to have one day a week when we act out the reality that ultimately our worth comes from being loved by God, not from what we do.

Our culture strongly links productivity with worth. It begins in childhood. Parents and teachers look at grades, test scores, awards and completed projects. Parents ask, "Were you good in school today?" Does anyone ever ask a child, "Where did you feel God's love today?"

> If we worry we are not good or whole inside, we will be reluctant to stop and rest, afraid we will find a lurking emptiness, a terrible, aching void with nothing to fill it.
>
> WAYNE MULLER, *SABBATH*

In some jobs, employees have to prove they have been productive in order to justify pay raises and promotions. We are taught to evaluate ourselves and others by external criteria. Does that man keep fit? Does that woman have a tidy home? Look at this front yard, all the weeds. These people must be lazy!

When we aren't being productive, we can find ourselves prey to all sorts of negative thoughts. Martha Whitmore Hickman describes our fear of unstructured time in her book *A Day of Rest*: "If I am not working, who am I? If I have free time, will my demons return—those thoughts and fears and possibilities that I am able to sidestep by being busy. Will I feel useless, uneasy? Will something *new* be expected of me?"

We receive messages over and over that we need to keep moving, get a lot done and prove we're okay. If we stop, the world might pass us by and we might miss out. The world's priorities of activity and productivity, which we adopt so easily, are one major obstacle to keeping a sabbath.

IDOLATRY

All this productivity and all these achievements can become a form of idolatry. We don't want to rest because we want to be indispensable. We don't want to stop being productive because our identities are rooted in activity and accomplishment. We want to make sure things are done well so that our work reflects well on us. Our culture encourages these behaviors and beliefs. It says nothing about how unhealthy it is to focus on work without a rhythm of rest built in. It says nothing about how our pride in productivity is a form of worshiping a false god.

One writer defends orthodox Jewish rules for the sabbath by saying, "When we cease interfering in the world we are acknowledging that it is God's world." By and large, most of us don't want to stop "interfering" in the world. We really don't want to acknowledge that the world belongs to God.

Dorothy Bass writes, "To act as if the world cannot get along without our work for one day in seven is a startling display of pride that denies the sufficiency of our generous Maker." The medieval church developed a list of the seven deadly sins, and pride was the first one. In fact, some people believe that all sins flow from pride. Embracing the sabbath helps us stand against pride. It helps us set aside our worship of our own achievements for one day each week and helps us know deep inside that the world is God's.

NOT GETTING ENOUGH DONE

Another obstacle to sabbath keeping is the perception that we don't work hard enough or have not accomplished enough to deserve a day off. This attitude is particularly common among people such as homemakers, students, independent contractors and retired people, whose work is self-directed or unstructured by an outside force. "I frittered the week away," a student finds herself thinking. "I intended to study almost every day, but I just didn't get there. I can't take a sabbath because I didn't work even close to six days."

Sometimes the way to get unstuck from procrastination and lack of self-discipline is to begin with a full day of enjoyable rest. Sometimes we are stuck in unproductivity because we have been trying to force ourselves to get things done day after day, with no break in our futile attempts at self-discipline.

Adam and Eve were created on the sixth day, so their first full day on earth was the seventh day, the sabbath. Then, on the next day, they began to till and tend the garden. They didn't begin to work until they had rested in God's presence. We often do the opposite, believing we have to earn the right to a day of rest by working hard.

LEGALISM

A father of two young daughters says, "I'm not too concerned about shopping or working on Sundays. I believe we should seek God every day. Also, if we have a relaxed family time on Saturday, and then need to work or do errands on Sunday, that's fine. I don't want to become legalistic and rule-based." His wife adds, "Having grown up in a church with a lot of rituals and rules, I struggle with grace versus legalism. I want to experience freedom from the law."

A teacher in her late twenties talks about the way her sabbath attempts moved toward legalism: "I tried to be intentional about observing a sabbath for about a year. I had a difficult time defining it for myself, sorting through what would be acceptable to do on the Sabbath and what would not. In some ways it became legalistic. In a strange way all the effort being put into rest and abstinence became stressful and hectic. I also found that it made Monday extremely frantic as I was trying to get everything together for the workweek."

Tony and Sara, a couple in their forties, are constantly aware of the battle to keep their sabbath from becoming legalistic. Tony says, "We observe a Sabbath in a very informal way, but it's very important to us. We try to avoid loading the day up with things that feel like work. I grew up around people who wouldn't let their kids play in the snow if it snowed on Sunday, so I fear legalism around this issue, but we certainly value the day of rest. I believe that we're made for it, because it doesn't feel right when we miss it."

I can identify with these concerns about excessive rules and legalism. When I was growing up, my mother often told the story of her father's childhood in a home with strict sabbath rules. My grandfather was born in the early 1890s, the first boy after eight girls. His father was a serious and committed Christian who believed that the only appropriate thing to do on Sunday was to sit still. Reading the Bible was all right, but not much else.

My grandfather died when I was eight, but I can clearly remember a vibrant man, full of jokes and laughter. He was easygoing, fun-loving and active. The sabbaths of his childhood were so difficult that he completely lost interest in the church. He felt he had sat still enough in his childhood to cover his whole life. The rules his father enforced did nothing to help my grandfather experience God's goodness and grace.

We enter into legalism when we focus on the letter of the law rather than its spirit. Over the years of the twentieth century, we abandoned sabbath rest in part because people experienced such distaste for strict obedience to the law. To avoid legalism as we experience the sabbath, we need to understand the purpose of the sabbath and keep that purpose clearly in mind as we develop structures and habits.

We also slide into legalism when we move toward the belief that we will be saved by what we do, when we think a particular behavior will earn God's approval. Grace teaches that there is nothing we can do to make God love us any more than he already does. Yet we humans are constantly tempted to believe God will like us more if we do certain things, and sabbath rules and regulations can open the door to this temptation.

Perhaps it was necessary over the course of the twentieth century to throw out many rigid sabbath rules in order to correct the imbalance toward legalism. Our desire for freedom can lead us in healthy directions, away from unnecessary regulations and tight structures. In our day, however, we need to rediscover the blessing of patterns and rhythms in time. We need to find freedom by embracing healthy discipline.

Enthusiastic sabbath observers often talk about the gift of the sabbath, the joy of stopping frantic activity to rest, celebrate and observe God's faithful hand. They are concerned about maintaining a weekly discipline that enables them to receive good gifts from God, a discipline that seems to splash grace over the other days of the week as well. Trying to earn God's approval appears to be the furthest thing from their minds.

Jesus' actions on the sabbath and his words about the sabbath communicate his desire for his followers to understand the spirit of the law. In Jesus' time, the joy of the sabbath was often lost because of the necessity of obeying all the rules with their specific details and minute distinctions. In our day, after the death and resurrection of Jesus and the coming of the Holy Spirit, we can keep the sabbath in a way that nurtures relationship with God and others. We can focus on the spirit of the sabbath law, God's call to rest in him with joy, focusing for one day each week on receiving his gifts.

Fear of legalism can rob us of the gift of the sabbath in the same way that our love of productivity can keep us focused on work without rest. Another obstacle to sabbath keeping is confusion about where to start.

WHICH DAY? WHAT TIME?

What is the best day to observe the sabbath? Saturday? Sunday? A weekday? If there isn't one right day, how can I know God wants me to do this?

Some people come from a Saturday sabbath tradition. These include people with a Jewish upbringing, Messianic Jews, Seventh-Day Adventists and Seventh-Day Baptists. If you come from one of these backgrounds, you may want to observe a Saturday sabbath.

Most Christians observe a Sunday sabbath for several reasons. Attending a worship service as part of the sabbath helps us focus on God and receive his gifts to us. Because Jesus rose from

> I don't think Sunday is the "right" day to keep as sabbath. I think each person needs to look at the rhythms of his or her week and decide what makes most sense.
>
> ANGELA, A WOMAN IN HER FORTIES

the dead on Sunday, every Sunday is the "Lord's Day," a small Easter, a day to remember the gift of the resurrection. Observing a sabbath on Sunday helps us celebrate the resurrection, to rejoice in our freedom in Christ.

However, some health-care workers, firefighters, security personnel, church workers and service professionals are not able to keep a sabbath on Sundays. They need to pick another day.

After you decide which day you will keep the sabbath, you also need to decide the time frame of your sabbath. Will you begin at sunset, so you can enter into the sabbath with candles and a celebratory meal? Will you set aside a day from waking to sleeping?

It really does take twenty-four hours to settle into rest, so don't cut the time short. Pick a beginning and end time based on what works for you and the people with whom you will be sharing the sabbath. You can experiment with the day of the week and time of day. You can experiment with what to cease doing and what to do. But whatever you try, give it at least three to six months so you can fully experience that particular pattern.

Our family's sabbath is sundown Saturday to sundown Sunday. It makes the change of seasons more interesting, to see how sundown moves through the year.

JANE, A MISSIONARY IN HER FORTIES

As much as possible, try to keep your sabbath on the same day of the week so you can develop a rhythm over the weeks and months. If you occasionally have to work on your regular sabbath, try to take a sabbath on the next possible day.

One student told me about friends of hers who, when they

had a spontaneous day of fun and relaxation, would say afterward, "I guess that was my sabbath for the week." While I affirm the need for spur-of-the-moment fun and a break from work, retroactively deciding on a sabbath day just won't work over time.

The sabbath is about rhythm, intentionality and expectation. We embrace a rhythm God designed, intentionally setting aside our work for a day so we can rest in the God who created and sustains the universe. We expect that this commitment to God's rhythm will teach us things about him, and we expect that we will experience his goodness in a way that transcends words. Spontaneous sabbaths are better than no rest at all, but the biggest gifts of the sabbath come over time through a consistent pattern of six days of work and one day of rest.

QUESTIONS FOR REFLECTION, DISCUSSION AND JOURNALING

1. In what ways do you embrace the rhythm of time affirmed in the Bible? In what ways are you able to thank God and rejoice in his goodness as you move through daily, weekly and yearly rhythms?

2. What fears do you have about unstructured time? In what ways do you need to be productive in order to feel worthwhile?

3. In what ways do you take comfort in rules or laws? Describe times you have embraced rules because you wanted to earn God's approval. Describe times you have obeyed rules in order to experience transformation through the Holy Spirit and nurture your relationship with God.

4. Identify the obstacles you experience to sabbath keeping.

PRAYING ABOUT THE SABBATH

Spend time praying about your fears of unstructured time, the ways you take comfort in rules and the obstacles you experience to sabbath keeping. Ask God to help you work through them.

CHAPTER SEVEN

Going It Alone

AND OTHER PRACTICAL ISSUES

So then, a sabbath rest still remains for the people of God; for those who enter God's rest

also cease from their labors as God did from his. Let us therefore make every effort to

enter that rest.

HEBREWS 4:9-11

When I first knew Andrea, she was working in a doctor's office, a job that seemed fairly people-intensive to me. Then she was hired by the sales department of a pharmaceutical company, and she began to travel frequently. Andrea, a single woman in her forties, is a people person, outgoing and friendly, but she experienced significant fatigue from her many interactions with people while traveling and selling her product.

Before she started the sales job, Andrea had always considered Sunday her sabbath, and she spent that day going to church and sharing meals with family and friends. When she began to experience fatigue from traveling, she started to observe a Saturday sabbath, spending the day entirely alone. After a few months of her new pattern, she could see the many benefits of solitude, something she had never allowed herself because she loved people so much.

Andrea's story illustrates one of the common patterns people face in their forties. Most individuals around that age find they enjoy time alone more than they did in the past. As I wrote in my earlier book, *A Renewed Spirituality: Finding Fresh Paths at Midlife*, a growing love of quiet seems to flower for many people in their forties and later, whether they are introverts or extroverts.

After a few years in sales, Andrea quit and went back to working in a doctor's office. Gradually her Saturday sabbath became a Sunday sabbath again. She still had meals with people on Sundays, but she also tried to spend time alone.

Andrea's story illustrates the reality that we may change our sabbath pattern over time. Her story also raises the question of sabbath observance all alone. Is it possible to keep a sabbath without support from family or friends?

CAN WE KEEP A SABBATH ON OUR OWN?

A friend of mine was listening to a rabbi talking on the radio about sabbath observance, and the rabbi insisted that the sabbath must involve community in some way. It is simply too challenging in our busy culture, he said, for anyone to think they can observe the sabbath by themselves—we need support in order to maintain such a countercultural discipline.

Some married people pursue sabbath keeping even though their spouse isn't interested. Some singles engage in a weekly sabbath without support from others. However, most people's experience reflects the rabbi's advice. The sabbath is best observed with others, in the support of a community.

Don Postema's thought-provoking book *Catch Your Breath* is designed to be used in six sessions of small group discussion. He believes we need to discuss with others our obstacles to sabbath keeping, even if we plan to observe a sabbath alone. Why is it so hard to rest? Why do we resist receiving from God? Together we can talk about the ways we need to refocus our lives as we experience sabbath rest. Together we can explore freedom in Christ, the release from captivity that we are invited to remember on the sabbath.

Postema also believes we can experience moments of sabbath as a group when together we enter a place of thankful receptivity to God's gifts. He believes that experiencing sabbath as a group will help us rest more fully on our own individual sabbaths.

The kind of companionship Postema describes can take place between husband and wife, parents and older children, friends, coworkers and members of a small group. Congregational leaders can encourage sabbath keeping among worshipers.

Support really does make a difference. If you desire to start a sabbath pattern in your life, find someone with whom you can share part or all of your sabbath day, or a friend with whom you can discuss the issues raised in your heart as you embrace the sabbath. Perhaps you will need to spend time alone on your sabbath, but you may enjoy gathering with others for a festive meal as the sabbath begins or ends.

> **We keep a sabbath for two reasons.**
>
> **First, to make time for God, to help our minds gravitate toward God as we spend a whole day trying to keep a commandment.**
>
> **Second, it's a fun day to look forward to all week.**
>
> JOHN AND KIM, A COUPLE IN THEIR THIRTIES

You may find stopping much harder than you anticipated, or you may find it delightful from the start. At first the day may drag. Your mind may not slow down. I can almost guarantee that something will surprise you when you start to keep a sabbath, and it helps to talk about what you are experiencing. You may need to brainstorm options for things to stop doing or ways to "play and pray." The sabbath indeed is countercultural, and we need support any time we make a strong stand such as this.

When you share a sabbath with a spouse, family members or roommates, you will certainly have to make basic decisions about when you will observe it, what you will do and not do. You may also need to discuss practical issues that seem inconsequential but may make or break the sabbath for you or your sabbath partner.

> During the times when we do observe the sabbath, we feel more connected to God and to each other. We always enjoy slowing down and having a day of rest, worship and reflection.
>
> MARK AND TARA, A COUPLE IN THEIR LATE TWENTIES

Ann, a single woman who has been observing the sabbath for more than thirty years, has shared her sabbath with various roommates, friends and vacation partners. She says her companions have had to learn that on the sabbath she does not want to be asked questions about work—they ruin the day for her. She has also negotiated with roommates about how to handle phone calls on the sabbath.

THE SABBATH FOR FAMILIES

Celebrating the sabbath as a family can bring great joy. Children usually enter enthusiastically into many aspects of sabbath observance. We found that our children wanted to know what sabbath meant, and they enjoyed reminding us of what we had said we wouldn't do. "You said you wouldn't mow the lawn on Sundays," they would point out when the weather cleared on a Sunday after weeks of rain.

Children love candles. Families who welcome the sabbath with a festive meal often report how much their children enjoy helping light the candles. Some families use one candle for each child or one for each family member, rather than the traditional two candles at the beginning of the sabbath.

Children also love receiving a blessing from their parents, a Jewish tradition that carries over very well into Christian families. A simple blessing works well, something like "May the Lord bless you today and every day of your life." One family gives their children their weekly allowance at the same time as they bless them on the sabbath to communicate that the sabbath is a time to celebrate.

Music is a great way to welcome the sabbath with children. One writer says the best investment she ever made was a set of rhythm instruments that her children used to welcome the sabbath when the family sang together. Children also enjoy a special meal, particularly if they can have a say in the menu.

For families who observe a sabbath on the same day as they go to church, getting to church can be a frantic business. To counteract this, parents can think about ways to nurture an atmosphere of peace—as much as possible—in getting ready for church. Let that morning preparation be part of a day of rest, luxury and abundance.

Consider which aspects of the morning rush before church are most stressful. Do the children argue about which clothes to wear? Invite them to choose their clothes on Saturday. Is breakfast too harried? Set the table the evening before, and prepare as much food ahead of time as possible. Is lunch a frenzied time? Make a casserole or soup the day before, or put a roast and potatoes in the oven before church with an automatic timer. Perhaps getting up fifteen minutes earlier would make a difference in everyone's stress level. The Jewish tradition of working before the sabbath can be a helpful guide. What can be done ahead of time? Analyze the sources of stress and think creatively, perhaps with a friend or a small group, about options for reducing stress.

The afternoon of the sabbath, after church, is a wonderful time to help children learn the Bible, perhaps in a new way or with special activities reserved for the day of rest. Some families act out Bible stories; others purchase Bible story coloring books that are saved for the sabbath. We talked earlier about a box for putting things away that won't be used on the sabbath. Some families create a different kind of sabbath box, one filled with crafts and games that are used only on this special day.

In *Making Sabbath Special*, Celeste Perrino Walker recommends making a "blessing box," a decorated box with a pad of paper and pencil attached. During the week, whenever anyone receives an answer to prayer or notices something they are particularly thankful for, they write down what happened and put it in the box. On the sabbath, the family reads the slips of paper together, taking time to discuss each one, then praying together and thanking God.

When children begin to have chores and homework, the sabbath is a day for them to cease from work just like adults. (However, they'll need help from parents to finish tasks ahead of time.) A day free from homework and chores benefits children because they can play uninterrupted for a long stretch of time. Parents benefit too because they don't have to do any reminding or nagging all day.

One family has a sabbath rule that no one can criticize anyone else on the sabbath. Not surprisingly, kids from other families love to come over on Sundays to experience a kind of peace that is missing the other days of the week.

No family should try everything described here. Doing so would be overwhelming and make the day feel like work. A couple of special activities for the sabbath can go a long way toward helping children understand that the day is set apart from the rest of the week.

Parents with young children face the danger of high expectations for their sabbath day as a family. They may have visions of a lovely family meal with singing and prayers, and children who have suddenly turned into angels. Just like anyone starting a sabbath observance, parents need to start small and consider what they most need to stop doing on the sabbath. Enjoy that permission to stop; revel in a day without housework or errands or yard work. Then later, add in a few sabbath habits to help your children engage and celebrate God's love and grace with you.

INTROVERTS AND EXTROVERTS

The question of how much time to spend alone on the sabbath is an important one for families as well as for people whose work makes special demands of them, such as Andrea from the beginning of this chapter. One man attends church on Sunday mornings, then spends the afternoon and evening with his wife's extended family. He loves those relaxed hours with adults and children. Since he works alone most of the week, Sundays provide a good balance of relational time after so much silence and quiet.

Andrea clearly needed lots of time alone on the sabbath while she was working at an intense sales job. Her need for a quiet day alone is common in our busy, harried time. Another woman, this one in her twenties, says:

> On Sundays, my husband I go to church then meet for lunch with a group of friends. We often spend the whole afternoon together. I love it because I love our friends, but I also find it exhausting. In our first year of marriage, we lived in another part of the country and spent Sundays alone together, just the two of us, after church. I miss that time, and I don't know how to get the time of quiet I need—by myself and with my husband—in order for Sundays to truly be a day of rest.

This woman is a self-proclaimed introvert, and most introverts need quieter, less social sabbaths than extroverts do for the day to feel restful. However, many extroverts who work in intensely relational jobs need a good deal of quiet time on the sabbath, while introverts who work alone often enjoy socializing during their day of rest. In order to set apart the sabbath for rest and provide balance with the other six days, we need to consider both our innate orientation to the outer world and what we do during the week.

> Because we do not rest, we lose our way.... We miss the quiet that would give us wisdom. We miss the joy and love born of effortless delight.
>
> WAYNE MULLER, *SABBATH*

SHOWING MERCY ON THE SABBATH

Jesus broke the sabbath laws of his time most often for the purpose of showing mercy to someone in need. Jews have long believed that showing compassion on the sabbath reflects the glorious abundance of the day. How can we exercise compassion on the sabbath without turning it into work?

We can answer that question in part by looking at our typical responsibilities. Teachers, nurses, counselors and people in many other professions show compassion as a significant part of their work. Perhaps they need to give themselves freedom from caring for people so they can experience rest. Or maybe they can show compassion on the sabbath in a way that differs from what they do during the week.

The sabbath is not a day to luxuriate in selfishness. On the sabbath, we rest from work in order to turn our hearts toward God, and God is always concerned with human need. Listening to God, being receptive to his gifts, noticing the beauty of creation almost always calls forth compassion in us. We can expect that turning our faces toward God will result in greater sensitivity to the places in our world where mercy is needed.

For those of us who have little opportunity during the workweek to exercise compassion, an important sabbath practice might be to visit someone who is sick or hold babies in the nursery at church. Yet we need to watch for compulsiveness. Are we showing compassion to feel better about ourselves? To try to earn God's love? Because we should? Or can we let God's presence and voice call us to show compassion because the love we have been given overflows from our hearts?

Whatever acts of compassion we choose to embrace on the sabbath, we can do them with care and attention. We can rejoice in small acts of caring and allow them to connect us to our compassionate God. I have begun to cook again on the sabbath in part because I want to show compassion for my husband, who comes home from work on Mondays depleted and hungry. Perhaps as I cook that dinner I can enter into Christ's compassion.

NURTURING TRANSFORMATION

Let's expand the questions above into the larger question of sabbath observance. Do I observe a sabbath to feel better about myself? To try to earn God's love? Because I should?

When we do something over and over, we are changed. When we exercise regularly, we become more fit. When we choose to express thankfulness consistently to God or the people around us, gratitude grows in our hearts. When we observe a sabbath with joy, over months and years our trust that God runs the universe increases. We become more aware of what we are called to do and not do. We rest in God's grace more easily.

A good motive for entering into a weekly day of rest comes from our desire for transformation. I choose to obey God because I long to be the person he created me to be. I have seen clearly that over time, my choice to draw near to God on the sabbath has changed my heart.

The goal of sabbath keeping is not to get it right the first time or even to get it right over time. Wayne Muller says that the point of adopting any habit is simply for the sake of doing it over and over:

> We have value beyond what we produce or achieve. In fact, we are accepted by God before we do or achieve anything important.
>
> DON POSTEMA, *CATCH YOUR BREATH*

We are not supposed to do it right the first time, and then be done with it. We are not supposed to do it better each year until we get it perfect. This year's Easter does not have to be new and improved, more dramatic and moving than last year's. The perfection is in the repetition, the sheer ordinariness, the intimate familiarity of a place known because we have visited it again and again, in so many different moments. Over the course of a lifetime there will be the sad Easter and the joyous Easter, the thoughtful Easter and the hopeful Easter, the transformative Easter and even the boring Easter. This is not about progress, it is about circles, cycles, and seasons, and the way time moves.

The same is true of the sabbath. Different sabbaths will feel sad, joyous, thoughtful, hopeful, transformative and even boring. "The perfection is in the repetition," Muller says. Eventually we will be able to enter into the familiar place of sabbath like coming home after a hard day's work and changing into comfortable clothes. We will be able to take a deep breath and relax into a different time, letting it be what it is—a gift, not one more thing to do or a ploy to make God love us more.

A SABBATH DAY VERSUS SABBATH MOMENTS

How do we get to the place where we can enter the sabbath as if we were putting on comfortable clothes? Like many writers on the sabbath, I recommend setting aside one whole day each week to experience rest. I believe in starting small in terms of what we cease from and what we do on the sabbath, but I do not recommend starting small in terms of time. The biblical sabbath of twenty-four hours is God's gift. It takes many hours to truly relax. My own experience with sabbath keeping began in Israel with a day that was dramatically different, so I see sabbath observance as deeply rooted in consistently keeping one day holy—which means separate or set apart—week after week.

Some writers and teachers recommend that we begin differently. They suggest that we experiment with sabbath time in smaller blocks. When we learn to stop striving and rest in God for shorter periods, they say, we will begin to be transformed and eventually desire a whole day of sabbath rest each week.

These writers and teachers draw on the contemplative Christian tradition, encouraging us to learn to breathe deeply, to pray in silence, to use ancient forms of contemplative prayer. They emphasize the necessity of stopping our frantic activity. They urge us to participate in music, art, poetry and other means of engaging the senses and imagination in an attitude of rest and refreshment in Christ.

Perhaps some people will find it easier to begin a sabbath observance by starting with small blocks of time. But I have two concerns. First, it often takes me a whole day before I have completely let down from my workweek. God gave us the twenty-four-hour sabbath for a reason. We need that much rest.

Second, the meaning of *sabbath* is "stop." First and foremost, we are called to stop doing things on the sabbath. If we immediately fill the time with other things, even things as good as contemplative prayer and poetry, we will be tempted to continue to focus on activity. During a short sabbath of an hour or two, we may be able to pray and engage with art or music for most of that time. During a twenty-four-hour sabbath, we will almost certainly not be able to do those activities the entire time. If we believe that every moment of sabbath time needs to feel spiritual or profound or significant, we will fall into the "shoulds" and "oughts" of legalism.

Still, the sabbath day does connect with sabbath moments during

As the body needs sleep every night, I believe our bodies, minds and spirits need a day of resting from labor. I believe the sabbath is a part of the cycle God intended in creation.

ELISE, A MINISTER IN HER THIRTIES

the week in a back and forth movement. Because I observe a weekly sabbath, I also experience sabbath moments at other times, moments that feel graced and holy and let me rest in God's goodness. The reverse is also true. I have learned many patterns of prayer and many ways of experiencing God's presence in daily life, and I bring them into the sabbath in ways that enrich the day of rest.

THROWING OUT PERFECTIONISM

In our time and culture, we face a significant challenge as we attempt sabbath observance. In ancient Israel, and even in our culture fifty years ago, the whole world stopped for a day. If we try to keep a sabbath now, in one sense we will be going it alone, even if we have support from family or friends. Our neighbors, and perhaps even our family, will be shopping and mowing lawns and working on their laptops because they view our sabbath as a workday.

In addition, some people who keep a sabbath will be shopping and mowing lawns and using their laptops on their sabbaths. The same activities that communicate God's rest and freedom to one person can feel like unhealthy self-indulgence or stringent legalism for another. We need to have a strong sense of inner direction, as well as support and encouragement from family or friends, in order to embrace this discipline.

We also must let go of the sense that we can do this thing perfectly. I have learned that I simply cannot be completely consistent in my sabbath observance. The sabbath is a day to nurture relationships, yet I spend most of it alone. In the past, my sabbaths involved time with my children, my husband and friends who came over for dinner. In the future, my sabbaths may include time with people again. But right now I do it alone, with great benefit. Is this too self-indulgent?

In general, I do not like to deal with money on the sabbath or require other people to work. Yet occasionally I shop or eat a meal out. We used to hire babysitters occasionally on the sabbath, even though that involved money and made someone else work, and it took away from our family time. I just can't do everything right on the sabbath!

But I have come to understand that my inconsistencies are part of the point. The sabbath is a day to let go of perfectionism and let God run the universe. On that day I will do my best to stop working, let God worry about what I'm not doing right, and rest in the joy of knowing him.

In this chapter we have considered many practical issues: the sabbath for families, spending the day alone or with others, avoiding legalism and perfectionism, showing mercy, and sabbath moments versus sabbath days. For some people, practical issues like these are so complex and challenging that they find themselves wanting to ignore the sabbath entirely. But facing practical challenges and experimenting with solutions for a workable sabbath will indeed bring good things into our lives. Finding rest in Christ gives great gifts no matter what form the rest takes.

QUESTIONS FOR REFLECTION, DISCUSSION AND JOURNALING

1. Who in your life might you approach with your feelings and

questions about sabbath observance? With whom do you want
to spend time on your sabbath?

2. What do you need on a day of rest: time alone or time with people? Both? In what proportions?

3. When you think about your current sabbath observance, or
   when you consider beginning to observe the sabbath, what are
   your motivations? How much do you desire to obey God's sabbath command in order to earn his love? To receive his love? To
   experience transformation over time?

4. What are your questions about the practical issues of sabbath
   observance?

PRAYING ABOUT THE SABBATH

Spend time praying about the connection between people and
the sabbath for you. Ask for God's guidance about whether you
need to be with people or alone. Ask him to guide you toward
the support you need if you are starting a sabbath or making
changes to your sabbath observance. In addition, pray about
your motivations.

CHAPTER EIGHT

Call the Sabbath a Delight

If you refrain from trampling the sabbath,

   from pursuing your own interests on my holy day;

if you call the sabbath a delight

   and the holy day of the LORD honorable;

if you honor it, not going your own ways,

   serving your own interests, or pursuing your own affairs;

then you shall take delight in the LORD,

   and I will make you ride upon the heights of the earth.

ISAIAH 58:13-14

While I was writing this book, about two dozen sabbaths came and went. Because I was spending significant time each week focused on the topic, my personal sabbaths received more scrutiny than usual. In addition, I found myself experimenting a little each week, trying new things, seeing how they felt.

One week I set out to shop for a specific item, something I do occasionally on my sabbath. I ended up running several errands as if it were a workday. I was seeing what it felt like to change my long-standing "no errands on the sabbath" pattern. I realized afterward that the day felt fragmented and yucky. I recommitted myself to shopping as seldom as possible on the sabbath.

On far too many of those two dozen sabbaths, I fell into the day in utter exhaustion. I had a few nice naps—I have to be completely spent in order to nap—but exhaustion makes reflection and prayer difficult. On those weeks I was deeply grateful that I had set aside a day for rest, because I don't know how I could have worked the next week without it. However, although the day still felt like a gift, the gift could have been richer if I had had the energy to be more attentive to God's presence. I realized that sabbath keeping is deepest and most satisfying when I am tired from a week of work, but not so exhausted that I border on catatonic.

> Keeping a sabbath doesn't guarantee serenity, but failing to keep it guarantees non-serenity.
>
> DONNA, A WOMAN IN HER FORTIES

For a couple months while I was writing this book, my sabbaths had a slightly compulsive feel. I filled them by reading with a level of determination I usually don't experience. I found it hard to take breaks, stare out the window and let my mind wander. At the end of those two months, I went on vacation and had lots of time to think and pray. I realized that I was fighting fear in a particular area of my life, and I had relentlessly filled the time on those sabbaths because I didn't want to acknowledge that fear. I didn't want to relax, reflect and let my inner-most thoughts surface. Once I had identified the fear and let it come into my conscious mind, I was able to relax again on the sabbath.

During these months of writing, I was a little uneasy and off balance as I paid so much attention to my sabbath patterns. The sabbath is meant to be experienced, not ana-lyzed. When we unwrap a gift, we experience the greatest joy if we thank the giver and then use the gift. Sitting around analyzing the gift—considering why the person chose it, how it reflects love or lack of love, whether we really want it or like it—keeps us from en-joying it.

> Sabbath is a sign of God's benevolent desire for the world. By observing the blessed sabbath, the world expresses gratitude to the God who calls us into flourishing life.
>
> RICHARD LOWERY, *SABBATH AND JUBILEE*

If you desire to begin a sabbath practice, make a plan and then follow it for three to six months, or perhaps even a year. Resist the temptation to analyze during that period; simply receive the gift of the sabbath. As much as you can, wait until the end of that time and then reflect on what you have experienced. Let the sabbath teach you.

Perhaps you will want to change your patterns of sabbath ob-servance. An attitude of experimentation is healthy, but don't try something new each week. Make a plan, let the weeks flow by, let fifteen or twenty or thirty sabbaths give you their gifts, and then stop to analyze and make changes.

In the twentieth century many Christians adopted a form of spirituality that began with knowledge. Study the Bible; learn the major precepts of the Christian faith; say the accurate and true things about God, Jesus, the Holy Spirit and the Christian life. This kind of spirituality asserts that after we have the basic truths straight, then we can begin living a life that honors God.

The sabbath works the other way around. It invites us to participate in something without totally understanding it. In fact, many faithful sabbath keepers say that only after years of observance did they begin to understand the profound lessons God was teaching them through it. Receive the gift of the sabbath over time. Embrace the sabbath without knowing everything you will learn from it.

WHY WE NEED THE SABBATH

Why is the sabbath so vital in our time? Don Postema uses five words to describe what happens on the sabbath: *rest, refreshment, receptivity, release* and *refocusing*. With the increasing pace of life, we are in desperate need of all five.

We need to learn how to rest, and the sabbath provides a practical, helpful framework in which to do just that. The sabbath invites us into rest for a long enough period that we can let down from our rapid pace and undone tasks. As we observe a sabbath, as we learn to stop moving so fast one day each week, we will be better able to stop for moments of rest during the other days as well.

We need to learn receptivity. All that we are, all that we have, comes from God. In truth, we receive everything and earn nothing. As our culture becomes more secular and as the pace speeds up, we easily fall into the trap of believing that what we have comes from our hard work. We are then in danger of missing the very heart of the Christian faith—the reality that God made us and loved us enough to redeem us. We need to build structures that put us in a position of receptivity.

We need release from that which enslaves us: possessions, productivity, pride, fear, anger, insecurity, unresolved pain, self-criticism and many other emotions and habits that master us. On the sabbath we are invited to experience release from these bonds, to step outside slavery for a day and rejoice in freedom. We have this freedom in Christ all the time, but we have a hard time experiencing it on this earth in fullness.

We need to refocus. Our rapid pace of life bears too much resemblance to a treadmill: constant activity that goes nowhere. We yearn to know where we are going and why. We need to explore our motivations and goals. A day each week with built-in reflection time goes a long way toward reclaiming our sense of direction and purpose.

> Through the chaos of everyday life
>
> the Sabbath shines like a beacon,
>
> pointing straight to God,
>
> reminding us that He is in control.
>
> He was in control at Creation,
>
> He was in control at the Cross,
>
> and our future is in his hands.
>
> CELESTE PERINNO WALKER, *MAKING SABBATH SPECIAL*

Don Postema's five words express some of the great needs of our time. The sabbath helps meet those needs.

GOD INVITES US TO NOTICE

We can also describe some of the significant needs of our age by considering the word *notice*. In order to live the kind of life God designed, we need to follow the commands and instructions in the Bible regarding being thankful, confessing sin, turning to God and serving him. In order to obey these commands, we need to notice things about our lives and respond appropriately. In order to notice, we need time to reflect, time to stop functioning.

We are called throughout the Bible to be thankful. How can we be thankful if we aren't taking time to notice what we've been given? The beauty of the earth, the food on our table, the people who express love to us, the satisfying aspects of our jobs, hobbies we enjoy—it takes time and reflection to realize how blessed we are by those gifts.

Even more challenging is noticing God's hand at work in the world. Perhaps I've prayed for something specific, and several weeks later I receive an answer. Am I aware that the prayer has been answered? Perhaps a relationship has turned around or a particular problem at work or in the family has completely disappeared. Have I noticed that God has been at work? In order to thank God for these gifts, we have to take the time to look back and observe that they have been given.

In order to draw near to God, we must know we need him. How can we notice our need for God if we have no time to reflect on the pattern of our lives? Unless we stop moving, we will not be able to notice the emptiness inside that can help us perceive our longing for God.

The Bible calls us to confess our sins (1 Jn 1:9). But unless we take time to notice the ways we fall short, we don't know what to confess. The Bible also calls us to "bear one another's burdens" (Gal 6:2). How can we do that if we don't consider what another person's burdens are and how God might be calling us to help carry them? We are instructed to "serve one another with whatever gift each of you has received" (1 Pet 4:10). In order to do this, we must know what our gifts are, which comes from reflecting on our lives and noticing how we find joy in serving.

Have you ever looked for animal footprints in the woods and tried to follow them? It takes concentration and stillness to find and follow tracks. Our lives will be immeasurably richer if we notice God's footprints in our lives, his fingerprints all over the events of our days. All this noticing takes time. We can and should pause each day to take time to notice, but we need more than moments.

The sabbath enables us to notice on a larger scale because of the length of time involved. Stopping work for a few minutes helps, but stopping for a whole day allows a quality of relaxation that brings refreshment, refocusing and receptivity in a profound way that a few minutes can't give. Over time the sabbath trains us to notice the hand of God because our own hands are still long enough for us to be inwardly changed.

> Today the heart of God is an open wound of love. He aches over our distance and preoccupation.
>
> RICHARD FOSTER

The sabbath teaches grace in a deep, experiential way. Perhaps more than anything else, in our time we need grace. We need to rest in the reality that our lives do not originate with us, that all love comes to us as a gift and that God's grace surrounds and fills us. God's love and favor come to us not because we deserve them but because of who God is.

Week in and week out, the sabbath calls us to experience that love and favor by resting in God. The sabbath frees us from the life-destroying forces in our world. The sabbath gives us an engaging rhythm, a musical beat, that helps us step away from advertisements and media and competition and stress one day every week.

Our culture encourages us to live 24-7, never stopping, never resting. God invites us into a live-giving cadence that we might, with a smile, call 24-6. Truly the sabbath is a gift for our time.

QUESTIONS FOR REFLECTION, DISCUSSION AND JOURNALING

1. Consider Don Postema's five words: *rest, refreshment, receptivity, release* and *refocusing.* In what ways do you need each of these in your life?

2. What do you need to spend time noticing? What would help you notice these things more easily?

3. In what areas of your life do you need to experience grace? freedom?

PRAYING ABOUT THE SABBATH

Spend time thanking God for what you are noticing right now about his work in your life and his gifts to you. Pray about the areas of your life in which would like to notice God's hand more carefully, areas in which you would like to experience grace and freedom. Pray about where you would like to go from here in your sabbath observance.

APPENDIX A

Some Jewish Sabbath Prayers

WHEN LIGHTING CANDLES

Blessed are you, Lord our God, King of the universe, who has set us apart by his commandments and commanded us to kindle the sabbath lights.

BLESSINGS OVER THE WINE OR JUICE

Blessed are you, Lord, God of all creation, creator of the fruit of the vine. Blessed are you, Lord, God of all creation, you have taught us the way of holiness through your commandments and have granted us your favor and given us your holy sabbath as an inheritance. This day is a memorial of Creation. It is a memorial of the breaking of the bonds of slavery and sin and death. Blessed are you, O Lord; you make holy the sabbath day.

BLESSING OVER THE BREAD

Blessed are you, Lord, God of all creation, you bring forth bread from the earth.

GRACE AFTER THE MEAL

Blessed are you, Lord our God, King of the universe, who fills the entire world in his goodness—with love, kindness, and mercy. He gives food to all people, because his kindness lasts forever. May the merciful God let us inherit the sabbath of the world to come, which will be a complete day of rest forever.

APPENDIX   B

For Further Reading

Bass, Dorothy. *Receiving the Day: Christian Practices for Opening the Gift of Time.* San Francisco: Jossey-Bass, 2000. 142 pages. One quarter of this Christian view of time covers sabbath keeping.

Dawn, Marva. *Keeping the Sabbath Wholly: Ceasing, Resting, Embracing, Feasting.* Grand Rapids: Eerdmans, 1989. 217 pages. One of the earliest and best-known books on sabbath keeping for Christians.

Edwards, Tilden. *Sabbath Time.* Revised ed. Nashville, Upper Room Books, 2003. 178 pages. A gentle and encouraging book with an emphasis on the Christian contemplative tradition.

Heschel, Abraham Joshua. *The Sabbath.* New York: Farrar, Straus and Giroux, 1951. 118 pages. An eloquent classic written by a Jewish scholar.

Hickman, Martha Whitmore. *A Day of Rest: Creating a Spiritual Space in Your Week.* New York: Avon Books, 1999. 132 pages. A straightforward and practical presentation of sabbath keeping for Christians.

Lowery, Richard. *Sabbath and Jubilee.* St. Louis: Chalice, 2000. 162 pages. A detailed and passionate discussion of the significance of the Old Testament sabbath and jubilee laws.

Muller, Wayne. *Sabbath.* New York: Bantam Books, 1999. 241 pages. Draws on traditions of rest in world religions and shows how sabbath keeping addresses many issues of our time.

Postema, Don. *Catch Your Breath: God's Invitation to Sabbath Rest.* Grand Rapids: CRC Publications, 1997. 93 pages. Six helpful meditations on aspects of sabbath keeping for Christians, designed to be discussed in groups.

Rubin, Barry, and Steffi Rubin. *The Sabbath: Entering God's Rest.* Baltimore: Lederer Books, 1998. 46 pages. Written by the leaders of a Messianic Jewish congregation, with Jewish traditions and prayers explained.

Walker, Celeste Perrino. *Making Sabbath Special.* Nampa, Id.: Pacific Press Publishing Association, 1999. 127 pages. Lots of practical ideas for Christian families and individuals.

Winner, Lauren F. *Mudhouse Sabbath.* Brewster, Mass.: Paraclete, 2003. Each chapter discusses one aspect of orthodox Judaism that the author misses in her new life as a Christian. One chapter addresses the sabbath.

Page 20:   "To fail to see": Leonard Doohan, *Leisure: A Spiritual Need* (Notre Dame, Ind.: Ave Maria, 1990), pp. 20-23.

Page 27:   Humans are infinitely necessary and infinitely superfluous: C. S. Lewis, *Perelandra* (New York: Macmillan, 1944), p. 217.

Page 27:   "When we do any kind of useful work": Richard Lischer, *Open Secrets* (New York: Broadway Books, 2001), pp. 145, 152.

Page 31:   "Ceasing, resting, embracing and feasting": Marva Dawn, *Keeping the Sabbath Wholly* (Grand Rapids, Mich.: Eerdmans, 1989).

Page 40:   Remembering versus observing the sabbath: Lauren F. Winner, *Mudhouse Sabbath* (Brewster, Mass.: Paraclete, 2003), pp. 8-9.

Page 41:   "It is understandable": Richard Lowery, *Sabbath and Jubilee* (St. Louis: Chalice, 2000), p. 109.

Page 43:   "Slaves cannot skip a day": Dorothy Bass, *Receiving the Day* (San Francisco: Jossey-Bass, 2000), p. 48.

Page 54:   "The sabbath is a day to abstain": Dawn, *Keeping the Sabbath Wholly*, p. 15.

Page 59:   Stopping the use of one machine: Wayne Muller, *Sabbath* (New York: Bantam, 1999), p. 27.

Page 62:   "Sabbath is a time to stop": Ibid., p. 137.

Page 63:   Quenching thirst with sabbath tranquility: Ibid., p. 126.

Page 66:   "We can refrain from activities": Bass, *Receiving the Day*, p. 65.

Page 73:   Queen and bride of the people: Dorothy Bass describes the sabbath as queen and bride of the people in Ibid., p. 49.

Page 76:   "The ability to experience something beautiful": Doohan, *Leisure*, p. 74.

Page 78:   "If we are to deeply and fully integrate": Muller, *Sabbath*, p. 151.

Page 81:   "Sabbath is much more than doing nothing": Stanley M. Hauerwas and William H. Willimon, *The Truth About God: The Ten Commandments in Christian Life* (Nashville: Abingdon, 1999), pp. 58-59.

Page 82:   "Good sabbath-keeping includes": Don Postema, expanding on Eugene Peterson's sabbath ideal of "pray and play," in *Catch*

Your Breath: God's Invitation to Sabbath Rest (Grand Rapids, Mich.: CRC, 1997), p. 71.

Page 83: Desire for a specific list: Walter Chantry, Call the Sabbath a Delight (Carlisle, Penn.: Banner of Truth Trust, 1991), p. 104.

Page 84: Rabbi's three questions: Celeste Perrino Walker, Making Sabbath Special (Nampa, Idaho: Pacific, 1999), p. 72.

Page 89: Busy, exhausted, empty: Jeff Marian, "Slow Down!" Faith@Work online devotional, July 22, 2003 <www.faithatwork.com>.

Page 94: "I tried doing sabbath": Postema, Catch Your Breath, p. 34.

Page 95: "If I am not working": Martha Whitmore Hickman, A Day of Rest: Creating a Spiritual Space in Your Week (New York: Avon, 1999), p. 36, 37.

Page 96: Interfering in the world: Winner, Mudhouse Sabbath, p. 7.

Page 96: "To act as if the world": Dorothy C. Bass, "Keeping Sabbath: Reviving a Christian Practice." Christian Century, January 1997, p. 15.

Page 105: A growing love of quiet: Lynne M. Baab, A Renewed Spirituality: Finding Fresh Paths at Midlife (Downers Grove, Ill.: InterVarsity Press, 2002), pp. 39-41.

Page 110: Forbidding criticism on the sabbath: Dorothy Bass and Craig Dykstra, eds. Practicing Our Faith (San Francisco: Jossey-Bass, 1997).

Page 114: "We are not supposed": Muller, Sabbath, pp. 89-90.

Page 122: Rest, refreshment, receptivity, release and refocusing: Postema, Catch Your Breath, pp. 27-84.

Page 127: Blessing for lighting candles: Barry Rubin and Steffi Rubin, The Sabbath: Entering God's Rest (Baltimore: Lederer: 1998), p. 16.

Page 127: Blessing over wine or juice: Tilden Edwards, Sabbath Time (Nashville: Upper Room, 1992), pp. 132-33.

Page 127: Blessing over bread: Edwards, Sabbath Time, p. 133.

Page 127: Grace after meal: Rubin, Sabbath: Entering God's Rest, p. 25.

About the Author

Lynne M. Baab is the author of many books and Bible studies. She received an M.Div. from Fuller Theological Seminary and served two Presbyterian congregations in Seattle as associate pastor and parish associate. In June 2007 she received a Ph.D. in communication from the University of Washington, and in July 2007 joined the faculty at the University of Otago in Dunedin, New Zealand, to teach pastoral theology. Her books for congregational leadership include *Beating Burnout in Congregations* and *Personality Type in Congregations* (published by The Alban Institute).

Visit Lynne's website <www.lynnebaab.com> to read interviews and articles she's written about topics related to her books.

Also by Lynne Baab

"This slender volume packs a surprising amount of content. . . . [W]ill help novice Christians dip in . . . and more seasoned practitioners become more creative and intentional."

Publishers Weekly, starred review

Written for individual or group use, the eight sessions in the LifeGuide® Bible study *Sabbath* will help you to learn more about what sabbath is and how to practice it.

Scripture Index